GHOSTS OF BERKELEY COUNTY, SOUTH CAROLINA

GHOSTS OF BERKELEY COUNTY, SOUTH CAROLINA

BRUCE ORR

PHOTOGRAPHY BY KAYLA ORR

Haunted America

Published by Haunted America
A Division of The History Press
Charleston, SC 29403
www.historypress.net

First published 2011

Manufactured in the United States

ISBN 978.1.60949.417.9

Orr, Bruce.
Ghosts of Berkeley County, South Carolina / Bruce Orr.
p. cm.
Includes bibliographical references.
ISBN 978-1-60949-417-9
1. Ghosts--South Carolina--Berkeley County. I. Title.
BF1472.U6O73 2011
133.109757'93--dc23
2011030453

Notice: The information in this book is true and complete to the best of our knowledge. It is offered without guarantee on the part of the author or The History Press. The author and The History Press disclaim all liability in connection with the use of this book.

For "Chief" Orr, my late father,
For "Skip," my stepfather,
For my brothers,
and
For my Uncle Thomas, the man who taught me how to tell a tale.

"Life's a journey, not a destination."
–Ralph Waldo Emerson

Then perhaps death in itself is just another part of the journey.

CONTENTS

Acknowledgements 11
Introduction 13

The Town of Childsbury and the Tale of Strawberry Chapel 17
Biggin Church of St. John's Parish 31
The Ghosts of Quenby Bridge 37
The Grave Robber and Benjamin Blackmon's Wife 43
Medway Plantation 47
The Old Goose Creek Church of St. James Parish 55
Captain "Mad Archie" Campbell's Wager 61
Hangman's Tree 65
Hags, Hants, Boo-daddies and Root Magic 71
Dickey Wants a Ride 79
Sheep Island Road and the Summerville Light 83
The Nazareth Cemetery and Headless Annie 91
The Plantation House at Wampee 95
Kecleh-Kudleh: The Cherokees' Hairy Savage 103
The Cherokee Legend of Spear Finger 111
The Ghosts of Camp Low Country and Richmond Plantation 115
Loch Dhu Plantation 117

Conclusion 119
Appendix: A Word to Would-be Ghost Hunters
and Artifact Collectors 121
Bibliography 125
About the Author and Photographer 127

Acknowledgements

I would like to take this opportunity to thank those people who helped me along the way in this endeavor:

The late M.C. Cannon, former sheriff of Berkeley County.
The late Johnny Richardson, former deputy sheriff with Berkeley County.
Sheriff Wayne Dewitt and my friends and associates with the Berkeley County Sheriff's Office.
The Library of Congress Prints and Photographs Archives.
Kayla Orr and KOP (Kayla Orr Photography) Shots.
The Berkeley County Public Library.
The Dorchester County Public Library.
The Charleston County Public Library.
The Henry Timrod Library.
The Berkeley County Museum.
Ray Bayless.
Rachel Bayless Smith.
Rick Presnell, owner of Swamp Fox Diving, and his sons, Erik and Alex.
Brooke and Jodie Haynie of Charleston Collegiate School.
Finally, the men, both those still here and those passed on, with whom I have had the privilege of hunting and fishing in my youth and who took the time to share a tale or two.

INTRODUCTION

Berkeley County, South Carolina, was established in 1682. It was named after John and William Berkeley, co-owners of the Province of South Carolina. It is the largest county in size in the state, covering a total area of 1,228 square miles. As of the Census of 2000, the population of the county was 142,651.

Often overshadowed by the city of Charleston, located in neighboring Charleston County, Berkeley County and its towns are often forgotten as historical landmarks. It has great historical significance, and its contributions helped form the nation in which we now reside. While historic Charleston was occupied by the British and under British rule, rural Berkeley County was the location of many skirmishes and battles in the fight for this country's independence. The swamps and wetlands of Berkeley County were ideal for hiding and concealment, and colonial leaders such as Francis Marion utilized them for "hit and run" tactics that they had learned from their interaction with the Native American tribes in the area. These types of attacks surprised and baffled the British forces. Francis Marion and his troops, dressed in drab woodland colors, would hide and ambush the British forces. In stark contrast, the British forces were easily spotted. The flash of highly polished metal on their uniforms and the sound of it clanking against itself alerted colonial troops of their presence. The bright white trousers and brighter red coats did not help them much either. It should not come as much of a surprise that this attire earned the British troops the nickname "Redcoats." Francis Marion's type of attacks and his ability to rapidly disappear into the dense swamplands of Berkeley County likewise earned him a nickname from his British adversaries: the "Swamp Fox."

In later years, after South Carolina seceded from the Union, the Confederacy also recognized the value of Berkeley County as a secluded location for covert operations. The Confederacy used Stony Landing in Moncks Corner to secretly build the "Little David," the first submarine in history to be successful in battle and to utilize a successful torpedo attack. While the CSS *Hunley* attracts attention in Charleston, the fact remains that if it had not been for its predecessor in Berkeley County, the CSS *Hunley* would have never existed. It is stories such as these that are often overlooked and more often overshadowed by Charleston. The same is true in regards to Berkeley County's ghost tales, folklore and legends.

My father was a retired chief in the U.S. Navy. We resided inside the boundaries of Berkeley County, just outside the town of Goose Creek. Throughout Berkeley County, my father was known simply as "the Chief." People who were unfamiliar with his naval background often asked him what he was chief of. His dark skin confused some, I am sure, and perhaps they thought he was referring to some Native American title that had been bestowed on him. At first my dad would often explain the naval connection, but as the inquiries continued (and failed to diminish), he became weary and developed a new response. He would simply respond, "I'm chief of the whole damn Creek!" He laid claim to being chief of the entire town of Goose Creek, and by the time he passed away in 1998 he was the "Chief of the Creek" to many in the area.

I often spent my springs fishing with him, summers working for him and falls and winters hunting with him. This allowed me to meet many interesting individuals who shared the tales of the area with a scrawny young boy who would one day be able to put them in a book for future generations.

In the early 1980s, I chose to enter the field of law enforcement. My father worked on and maintained the patrol vehicles for the Berkeley County Sheriff's Office. When I told him of my intentions, he took me to see Sheriff M.C. Cannon, and together they spent more than an hour trying to talk me out of it. I was twenty years old. In the end, they were unable to sway me, and M.C. told my father that he would make me a jailer inside the jail and that if I survived until I was twenty-one, the age required by the state for certification, he would make me a deputy.

I survived and M.C. kept his word. When I turned twenty-one, he made me a deputy, and his captain, future sheriff Wayne Dewitt, presented me with my first badge as I was sworn in. It was the beginning of a long and rewarding career, and although I finished my career in another county under another sheriff, named Cannon, I never forgot that hour in M.C.'s office or where I came from.

I have since retired from law enforcement and returned to Moncks Corner and Berkeley County, where I reside. They say you can never go home again. That, my friends, is a lie. I have returned home, where I will live out the remainder of my life. Perhaps after I am dead and gone I will stay a little while longer. I would love to stomp about and slam doors at 3:00 a.m. I would pay my children back for all the door slamming that they did in their teenage years.

Speaking of teenagers, I recently had the pleasure of assisting my good friend Rick Presnell on a scuba diving trip to Florida. He was certifying a group of high school students from Charleston Collegiate, and I attended as a safety diver. After diving all day, we would gather together at night around the campfire and share our experiences of the day, as well as an occasional ghost tale or two. As the students expressed their excitement at seeing American bald eagles and Florida manatees, I could not help but think about the fact that these creatures have been brought to the brink of extinction and, without preservation efforts, would be lost to future generations. Rick and I also discussed the fact that many of the places we hunted and fished as kids have now been lost to residential and commercial construction. As kids we took for granted that they would always be there. Sadly we were wrong.

I greatly admire the two teachers, Brooke and Jodie Haynie, who worked so hard at creating a program that allowed their students to have such a unique and wonderful experience above and below the water. The students diligently worked toward their scuba certification under the guidance of the Haynies. It is an experience that they will take with them for a lifetime.

I also thank the two teachers for a lesson that they taught me on this trip. Through this trip and all of our interaction during this excursion, it created a realization in all of us that without preservation many things we take for granted would be lost—like folklore and legends, for example.

Ghosts of Berkeley County, South Carolina is a collection of the tales indigenous to the area in which I grew up. You may find some of these tales scattered throughout other ghost books of South Carolina, but you will not find another collection dedicated solely to this area. These are the stories that were told to me by my family and also by the people my father introduced to me. Also included with those tales are some newer legends that I have located in additional sources through the years. As I have stated in my previous books,

I am not here to convince you that ghosts, goblins and ghouls do exist. I am also not here to dissuade you from your beliefs if you do believe in them. I am simply presenting a compilation of local legends and tales for your entertainment and the entertainment of future generations. You the reader can draw your own conclusions as to what you choose to believe.

I mentioned Rick Presnell earlier. When I was a sergeant assigned to the Homicide and Violent Crimes Division, he was the sergeant over the Technical Service Unit and Crime Scene. We both have since retired and spend a great deal of time scuba diving together. It is a drastic contrast to what our careers brought us together to face. We know a great deal about death—perhaps far more than we care to. The other day, as Rick and I were relaxing after another brief dive trip, the song "Amazing" by Aerosmith popped up, and as Steven Tyler sang the lyrics, one line stuck with us and taught us a lesson about death we never considered: "Life's a journey, not a destination."

Perhaps death in itself is not the ending of life that we once thought it. Maybe death is, quite simply, another part of the journey.

THE TOWN OF CHILDSBURY AND THE TALE OF STRAWBERRY CHAPEL

Perhaps the most famous legend from Berkeley County is that of Strawberry Chapel and Catherine Chicken. James Child founded the town, along with French Huguenots, in 1707. The Huguenots were members of the Protestant Reformed Church of France. The town has been described as an apex of commerce along the Cooper River. It was once a thriving and bustling community and a historic example of the interactions between Native American, African American and Euro-American cultures. Strawberry Ferry had been built two years earlier at this strategic location and served to connect the communities by creating a means of shipping and transportation. The Carolina colony had only been in existence for twenty-five years before the ferry was built, and then, two years later, James Child mapped out 185 lots on one hundred acres and created a town that would eventually consist of the ferry, a free school, a tavern, a general store, a chapel and a racetrack. The location also contained the wrecks of two British ships that were captured along with a large number of British soldiers by Colonel Wade Hampton during the Revolutionary War. The military sloops were plundered and then burned and scuttled. They sank near Strawberry Ferry. Underwater archaeological artifacts can still be located under the Cooper River in the surrounding area. The diversity of the evidence shows that many different cultures had an influence on the town of Childsbury.

Archaeological evidence shows that Native Americans also resided in the town and traded deerskin with the settlers. The Cherokees were believed to have traded the skins that were transported down the Cooper River and

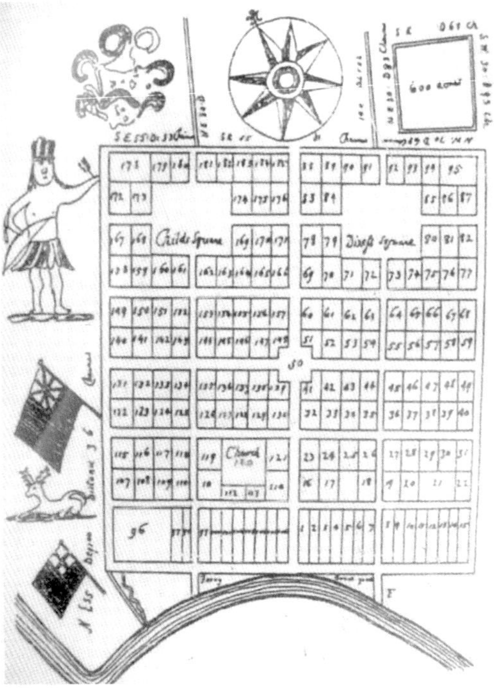

Left: Map of the town of Childsbury, hand drawn by its founder. *Courtesy of KOP Shots.*

Below: A brick believed to have been used as ballast in one of two British sloops burned during the Revolutionary War. *Courtesy of Swamp Fox Diving.*

sold in Charles Towne. Colonoware, pottery made by African American slaves found at the site, also illustrates the influence of African culture on the community. We know that from 1708 through the eighteenth century, the majority of South Carolina's population (outside Native Americans) was black. St. James Parish in Goose Creek alone had 2,027 African slaves to 535 whites. The town, as stated earlier, had quite a diversity.

The Strawberry Chapel was constructed about 1725 as a chapel of ease to give the town a place of worship without the parishioners having to travel ten miles away to Biggin Church. There is also a small brick pit covered with an arched roof that was built adjacent to the church. This pit was used to store and give shelter to coffins and their occupants during inclement weather while waiting to be interred there or moved down the river to Biggin Church. The town continued to be used until the 1750s, when a malaria epidemic is believed to have wiped out the remaining population of the town. The little brick and stucco chapel is all that remains of the settlement.

The only remaining story is that of Little Mistress Chicken. It has been retold throughout the centuries but was fortunately recorded in book from about 1913 by Mrs. Arthur Gordon Rose.

Strawberry Chapel, the last remaining structure of the town of Childsbury. *Courtesy of KOP Shots.*

The author examining a covered pit used to protect coffins from inclement weather prior to burial. *Courtesy of KOP Shots.*

Catherine Chicken was the grandchild of Childsbury founder James Child. Her mother was Lydia Chicken, and her father was the late Captain George Chicken. He had been the commissioner on Indian affairs for the province and a member of the Goose Creek militia. He had been involved in driving the hostile Yemasse Indians out of Carolina and down into the Everglades of Florida.

Catherine's mother had remarried the year before to Elias Ball of Kensington Plantation. Catherine had been sent to boarding school at Childsbury and placed into the care of Monsieur and Madame Dutarque. The move had been extremely hard on the child, and the separation from her mother after the loss of her father was even worse on the seven-year-old girl. The fact that she now had a baby sister, Elizabeth, whom she had never met, was even worse.

The Dutarques were extremely harsh individuals. One day, Madame Dutarque gave the child a garment to sew as punishment. What by today's standards would be considered normal separation anxiety and taken into consideration by school administrators was deemed to be laziness by Catherine's educators.

The child missed her mother and grandfather. She had been raised on Luckins Plantation, several miles away. She missed the animals and the pets she left behind. She missed her kittens and puppies. She missed the Chickasaw pony she left behind. She had pleaded to be able to bring them with her but was told that Monsieur Dutarque despised pets. She did manage, however, to conceal a small turtle and bring him with her. Her stepfather had named the little turtle Flying Childers after a very fast local racehorse. He thought it was amusing because the turtle was so slow.

The day of her punishment, Catherine was extremely homesick. She placed the turtle on the ground, and he began to take off as fast as a turtle can. She dropped the linen that she was supposed to sew and chased after the turtle in a game of cat and mouse in the grass and underbrush. She eventually wandered away from the schoolhouse and down through the town. With the tiny turtle in hand, she sat down under a very large live oak tree and forgot all about the linen she was to sew and the Dutarques. She was caught up in memories and thoughts of her family and home, and she watched the boats moving in and around the ferry.

Eventually, she remembered the linen and her punishment for being lazy. She searched for it, and when she saw that it was missing, she came to the realization that she would get in trouble again. She thought about running away and finding her way back to Luckins Plantation, but the fear of getting lost, eaten by a bear, scalped by an Indian or attacked by a ghost kept her from carrying out any escape attempts. She also realized that it would soon be dark. She had not meant to be away this long from the schoolhouse and actually had not meant to leave it at all. She had been so caught up in her thoughts that she did not even realize that she had wandered off until it was too late. She rose from her place under the tree and turned to walk back to the schoolhouse. She was startled as she looked up and saw the face of the one person she did not want to see: Monsieur Dutarque.

The schoolmaster had been interrupted from his study of Plato by the screams of his wife. She had discovered that Catherine was missing and, after searching everywhere, became extremely alarmed. She then alerted her husband to the disappearance. The concern and alarm was not for the missing child because, in actuality, neither of them cared about Catherine. What they were most concerned with was the fact that Elias Ball had placed her in their care, and he, along with many of the child's relatives, was very influential in St. John's Parish and in the entire province. They were concerned with what would happen to them if something might happen to the child. Now that dinnertime had come and gone without sign of the child, he knew that he would have to extend the search to outside of the schoolhouse.

Monsieur Dutarque had grown very angry. He was underpaid, and although he carried the credentials to be the schoolmaster, he was a man who despised children. To say he was unfit to be the schoolmaster would be an understatement. The man had armed himself with his horse pistols and a great length of rope and had set out to search for the missing child. The Dutarques agreed not to sound the alarm until after he had made a search of the town. If he could not find the child, then the two of them would sit down and conceive of some elaborate lie to remove the focus of blame from themselves.

As Monsieur Dutarque began his search, he stumbled across the linen that the child had been given to sew. His heart jumped into his throat as fear gripped him. He knew that something horrible had happened to the child and that made him smile, but then the pleasure was short-lived as he realized that he would surely be hanged. He was at a section of town known as Colledge Square, where the markets assembled just outside the ferry. Just as he was about to give up on the child and begin creating a story of her falling into the river, the little imp rose up from behind a tree. The schoolmaster's fear turned to anger. His anger then turned to rage.

He would have loved to have beaten her with a whip as he had done to the slaves he had been overseer of in a faraway parish. He had concealed this and many other facts of his life from those who had employed him. He truly wished he could inflict the pain on the child that he had inflicted on so many slaves. Inflicting pain had always given him so much pleasure.

He reached down and snatched the child by the arm and shook her. "Sacrebleau!" he hissed. "What mean you naughty, willful wench! Do you know what hour of the day it is? What am I to say to Madame, your mother?"

Catherine's lip quivered. She tried to answer that she had meant no harm, but it all broke out in one feeble, sobbing, childish cry: "I wanted to be outdoors! I wanted to be outdoors!" "Aha! Outdoors, is it?" said the angry schoolmaster. "Outdoors? I myself will give you enough outdoors Mademoiselle. Outdoors—parbleu! She shall haf outdoors, vraiment!" In his wrath, the excellent English of the schoolmaster had momentarily escaped him. Straight up Ferry Street he dragged her, she making no resistance, and along Church Street as far as the wicket gate made in the cedar fence. The grip on her arm was like iron, and they met no one to whom Catherine could call to deliver her from her angry captor. She kept Flying Childers tightly clasped, glad in her extremity that her pet would suffer without a sound. What was Monsieur Dutarque about to do with her?

He knew he could not strike her, so immediately he contrived another form of punishment. With the rope he had carried he bound Catherine tightly with her back against a tombstone, her hands behind her and her shoulders strained back with cruel knots. "V'la!" he said, pausing to look at his work. "You s'all haf yo' outdoors! And ven you s'all be fatigue, you may call. Maybe I come."

In adjusting the final knot, he noticed her tightly clenched hand and forced it open. There he saw the turtle Flying Childers hidden there. He snatched it away from her and bashed the helpless creature against the tombstone with all his might, killing it in front of the horrified child. Stepping back and admiring his work, he let out a light chuckle and then walked away, ignoring the child's pitiful pleas to release her and not leave her.

The child struggled to free herself but was unsuccessful. Her screams and pleas drifted off into the night. The more she struggled the wearier she became and the more faint her pitiful cries became. A neighbor, James Macnamara, heard the cries and originally thought they were from an owl. As he listened, he thought that they sounded like Catherine Chicken. He left his house and called out but had no response. He had an uneasy feeling, and he went to see the Dutarques. They informed him that Catherine was staying with her aunt, Hannah Harleston. There was something not right about how the Dutarques were behaving, and Macnamara returned to get his horse and rode out to the home of Catherine's aunt. When he learned that she was not there and his suspicions were confirmed, half the countryside was alerted. In the meantime, the Dutarques had no idea what was taking place, and the exhausted Catherine had passed out from her struggles and the overwhelming fear she was feeling. It is unimaginable to even begin to comprehend the utter terror that the seven-year-old child was experiencing at being tied to a tombstone inside a graveyard and left there in the dark. Catherine had been tied standing up and, now quite weary, had cried herself to sleep and was hanging painfully from her restraints.

In those days, there were curfews for the protection of the citizens of Childsbury. There were also strict laws regarding the slaves of the town. One slave, known as Money, happened to be out past the curfew. He was in fear of his life, so he had constructed a device to scare anyone away who might approach. He had taken a gourd and carved a grotesque face in it. He then placed it on top of a long pole and put a candle inside it. The hideous face would be mistaken for a demon, and anyone approaching

A cemetery near Strawberry Chapel, where Catherine Chicken was left tied to a tombstone. *Courtesy of KOP Shots.*

would be frightened away, especially since he was taking a shortcut through the cemetery.

As Money walked through the cemetery, Catherine awakened. The first thing the poor child saw was the demonic face burning eight feet above the ground and coming in her direction. The child let out a terrified scream and fainted. Money also screamed and dropped the gourd. As he turned to flee, he saw the child suspended from the tombstone.

Money now faced a dilemma. Should he get help for the child and risk being beaten for being out past curfew, or should he leave her there and hope that she would be found? Soon the area was filled with the sounds of men, dogs and horses already searching for the child. At that moment, Money decided that the child had never done anything to anyone and did not deserve the fate she was suffering. As a slave, he could relate to the child. How often had he been tied and beaten for something trivial or something he had no control over? Too many was the answer.

As the slave began to move toward the men, Catherine cried out in a pitiful voice, "Monsieur Dutarque, why did you leave me here." The slave immediately realized that the schoolmaster had been the culprit and had left the child there. He immediately ran to the men and told them of his discovery. Catherine was cut down and taken away to be seen by the physician. The mob then turned its focus on the Dutarques. They were dragged from their beds and held captive in the schoolhouse, with James Macnamara standing guard. Many called for their hanging by the same rope the child had been bound with, but many more understood that the law should handle the matter.

The next day, it was determined that the child might not live, and her face was drooped with palsy. She was also speechless, and although it was obvious that she was having nightmares, she never uttered a word. The anger in the town grew as preparations for a hearing were made. Several days passed, and the child remained bedridden. It was feared that the child might never awaken.

On the very day of the hearing, Catherine awoke. She looked into the face of her mother and faintly mumbled, "Please don't let them hurt poor Monsieur Dutarque." The child, while unconscious, had undoubtedly been able to hear others speaking of Dutarque's fate. She then requested her turtle.

Word was relayed to the tribunal of young Catherine's request. Elias Ball had sent out a hunting party to find a replacement for the deceased pet, and when a passable substitute was found, he had it delivered to the child. He also told the gathering crowd of the child's request for mercy. When he told the crowd that it was to be honored, there was a great cry of disbelief. Many claimed that it was an injustice, yet Elias Ball stood firm.

Ball had Madame Dutarque escorted to the ferry and carried across the river, where she was deposited on the shore. He then turned his focus on Monsieur Dutarque. Elias Ball went over and whispered into Money's ear. The slave grinned, walked over and grabbed Dutarque. He was stripped of his clothing down to his undergarments and then bound and placed on a mule, facing backward. The drummer boys of the militia were then gathered together and lined up behind the mule. Monsieur Dutarque was then escorted through town to the sound of the beating drums. The mule kicked and turned, and laughter arose from the crowd. Many gathered rocks, fruits, eggs and whatever they could find and pelted the former schoolmaster as he passed. He was then escorted down to the ferry and taken across the river. The mule was then struck with a whip, and it bolted off into the woods, carrying Monsieur Dutarque with it. Elias Ball had honored Catherine's wishes, and no one in town harmed Monsieur Dutarque. He could speak for the town, but he could not speak for the bears, alligators and hostile Indians on the other side of the Cooper River. Dutarque had been drummed out of town, and his fate was left up to God much as he had left Catherine's.

Catherine recovered eventually. She always bore the drooped expression from the palsy that the trauma had inflicted on her. She grew into an adult and married Benjamin Simmons of Middleburg Plantation. It is also said that the slang term "being chicken" (feeling and expressing fear) was derived from Catherine Chicken's ordeal.

It is said that after death Catherine returned to the home in which she grew up. Luckins Plantation burned to the ground, and Rice Hope Plantation was built where it stood. Catherine's spirit has apparently reverted back to a child, and she can be heard calling for her family and wandering about the house. The place has been converted into a wonderful bed-and-breakfast and has been operating as such since 1987. The Heron Room, the room that overlooks the river, is said to be the place where Catherine is most active. There used to be a rocking chair in the room that would continually rock the entire night. It has since been removed and relocated to another area of the house.

Catherine is also said to haunt Strawberry Chapel, where she was bound and left. Her cries for help are said to be heard at night. The chapel and its grounds have been the subject of repeated vandalism and have been closed to the public. Permission must be granted before entering onto the property because trespassing laws are enforced by the sheriff's office.

As far as Monsieur Dutarque, he managed to escape death and find his way to Camden, South Carolina, where he became the French teacher for the Walnut School for Boys. He had carried with him an outdated letter of recommendation from a school he had taught at in New Orleans. He had carefully cut away the date. The citizens in Camden were excited to have a new French teacher and knew nothing about Monsieur Dutarque's problems at Childsbury. The fourteen boys initially marveled at the tales Monsieur Dutarque told them of his travels abroad. When the inquiries became too personal for Dutarque's taste, he had them rephrase the question in French. This worked well, and eventually he had the students only speak to him in French, although he spoke to them in English. This greatly diminished any chance of having to converse with the students in great detail, much to the teacher's delight.

One day, the boys entered the schoolroom and found Monsieur Dutarque missing. They waited for more than half an hour. Eventually one of the students asked the others if they heard a dripping sound. As they investigated,

Rice Hope Plantation, formerly Luckins Plantation, where Catherine Chicken is said to haunt. *Courtesy of KOP Shots.*

they discovered that the dripping was coming from Monsieur Dutarque's desk. They discovered a huge pool of blood on the desk next to the final exams they had taken the previous day. One of the students, Jonathan Charles Fort, lifted his exam from the top of the stack. Every answer on his test was marked with a big bloody "X," and at the top it was marked with the letter "F," in blood. He handed out all of the tests to the respective students. Each one had been graded and scored an F. Every single paper had been graded in blood by Monsieur Dutarque.

Apparently, he had not learned his lesson at Childsbury. In the months preceding the final exam, the schoolteacher had taken to being verbally abusive toward his students. The student often gathered at the well that served the schoolhouse, and he would approach the group every morning and begin chastising them about their appearance, their families and their lack of ever amounting to anything other than dirt farmers. He would point his finger in their faces and shake his fist. A multicolored bead bracelet he always wore, yet never spoke of, would rattle with every gesture. He would select a student to raise and lower the bucket as he drank his fill. The boys

Monsieur Dutarque finally met poetic justice at the bottom of a well many miles from Childsbury. *Courtesy of KOP Shots.*

began to suspect that his overwhelming thirst for water had something to do with his overwhelming thirst for red wine the night before. This routine continued every morning until this morning, when the teacher had turned up missing.

No one knew what happened to the teacher, and speculation grew as to what may have happened. As the boys left for the harvest season, the school remained abandoned.

Eventually, the boys returned to the school, and as usual they gathered around the well in the morning. One of the boys noticed that the bucket was lowered into the well, and he attempted to retrieve it. He tried with all his might, but the bucket would not budge. Another boy grabbed on to the lever, and the two tried to turn it with all their strength. Eventually, the bucket broke free, but it had an unusual weight to it. They continued to turn the crank until the bucket slowly rose to the service and revealed, much to their horror, the cause of its added weight.

As the bucket rose to the top, it revealed the partially skeletonized torso of a human being. The skull contained remnants of black hair, and on the wrist was a multicolored beaded bracelet. It was the remains of the missing schoolteacher. Apparently, after grading the tests while in a drunken state, he had wandered out to retrieve water from the well. Obviously the inebriated man had lowered the bucket and then fallen into the well on top of it and had drowned. Justice had finally reached Monsieur Dutarque—grading the papers in blood was the last cruel act Dutarque ever committed against a child. He had died in the manner he had prepared to use as the excuse for Catherine Chicken's disappearance. He had fallen in the well and drowned.

Biggin Church of St. John's Parish

I have heard many tales about the church on Biggin Hill, but one of the more recent and intriguing ones involved a man named Jacob Skelen and his encounter with the church in 2004. According to the story, Skelen had made a recent move, and within the first week he had begun receiving the assorted junk mail marked "current resident" that accompanies every move and postal change. As he was sorting the mail, one particular envelope caught his eye. It was aged and brittle. It was also sealed with wax that flaked off as soon as he touched it. The return address was marked Biggin Episcopal Church, St. John's Parish, South Carolina. There was no zip code.

Skelen was intrigued and opened the letter. Inside he found an equally old and brittle letter. He carefully unfolded it to find that it was handwritten in an indigo-colored ink. As he held it up, he saw the image of the face of Jesus, eyes closed and a crown of thorns encircling his head. The accompanying note told him to use the paper as a prayer rug, to kneel on it and pray from the book of Psalms. It advised that if he did so, he would see his prayer planted and harvested. The next line advised that the image of Christ would awaken after he had done so and then again looked directly at the image. Skelen's curiosity was aroused, and he did as he was instructed. After reading and praying from the book of Psalms, he again looked at the image. This time, the image's eyes were wide open and staring back into his own eyes. Startled, he dropped the paper as if it had bitten him.

The young man laughed and retrieved the paper. He then again peered at the image from all angles and reasoned that it had been the trick of some well-crafted watermark on the page. He finished reading the letter, which instructed him to write a prayer request, place the request and the letter back into the envelope, enclose an offering of his choice and mail it back to Biggin Episcopal Church. It ended by saying that Jesus would hear and honor his request and send the Holy Spirit to pass by his window that night.

Skelen was very skeptical. He was a man who would not believe in anything that he could not see, but a spirit outside his window would undoubtedly change his opinion, he thought to himself.

The next morning, Skelen could not recall anything unusual occurring in the night. As he prepared for the day, he again thought of the mysterious letter. As a joke, he decided to respond. On a note, he simply wrote that he wished to experience a ghost. It did not have to be the Holy Ghost—any ghost would do. He again surmised that any actions taken by any ghost would change his mind toward the things of this world that he could not see. He then laughed and tossed the envelope in the mail slot as he left.

In the following months, he forgot about the letter he had received until one night in December, when he returned home to find a similar envelope halfway under his door. This time the letter contained two coins attached to it in a crumbling yellow wax. The letter informed him that his prayer had indeed been heard. It further informed him that the Holy Spirit had indeed seen him that night as it passed by his window. The letter also advised him to place one coin in his left shoe for all blessings past and one coin in his right shoe for all blessings yet to come. The past and the present would soon merge. The letter advised him to read from the twenty-eighth chapter of Deuteronomy and send his request back to the church. It asked him to keep the coins in his shoes the following day and then place one shoe inside his door and one outside his door that night.

This was insane, thought Skelen, yet once again the young man did as he was instructed. This time he quickly wrote a request for money, reversed the address on the letter and threw it in the mail slot. He did as instructed the next day, and that night he placed one boot containing a coin inside his door and another outside the door. He slept very little. He kept checking the boots. The next morning, nothing had changed. He went back to his daily routine. That evening, he received a flyer in the mail telling of an antique coin show in Charleston. He wondered at the coincidence and retrieved the coins. As he examined them, he saw that they were unusual in the fact that they were stamped "Confederate States of America 1861." He had not noticed this before.

The day of the coin show, he took the two pennies and hurried off. When he arrived, he had the coins inspected and was astonished to find that they were rare mint Confederate coins made by Robert Lovett Jr. He had been commissioned by Philadelphia jewelers Bailey and Company. At the show, the rare coins sold for more than $5,000 per coin. With more than $10,000 in hand, the elated young man was determined to attend the church and thank them. He told the antique dealer of his intentions. The man just laughed and advised him that doing that would be extremely difficult. He then told him that the church had been destroyed by fire in the late 1800s. Skelen knew the man had to be mistaken. He had to see for himself.

After receiving directions, he drove to the location and was shocked at what he saw. There was nothing left of the church but a few walls and a cemetery, just as the coin dealer had described. He searched the grounds and found a historical marker that confirmed that the church had been destroyed by fire in 1886 and never rebuilt after that. Skelen was overcome. Not only had his last request for money been granted, his first request to experience a ghost had also obviously been granted.

Biggin Church was originally built in 1712 as an Anglican church by a missionary minister named Robert Maule. He was assigned to Saint John's Parish by the Church Act of 1706 that created ten parishes in the province. The site was named after Biggin Hill in Kent, Great Britain. It served the parish of St. Johns and was the church used by the town of Childsbury until Strawberry Chapel was constructed as a chapel of ease for the residents who were unable to make the ten-mile trek to Biggin Church.

Just as Childsbury seemed to be cursed and died out after the events involving Catherine Chicken, so did Biggin Church. It was a church destined to burn. In 1756, it was destroyed by a raging forest fire. The parishioners rebuilt the church in 1761, but in 1781 it was again burned to the ground by British forces. The church had been seized by the British under the command of Colonel Coates and had been utilized as a weapons and ammo depot. When colonial troops advanced, Coates ordered the church and any remaining supplies to be burned to prevent them from falling into rebel hands. The British then retreated back to British-occupied Charleston.

After the Revolutionary War, the parishioners again rebuilt the church. When the Civil War began in 1861, the church was stripped of its pews

Above: The ruins of Biggin Church, where Jacob Skelen realized that his prayer to meet a ghost had been answered. *Courtesy of KOP Shots.*

Below: Biggin Church seemed destined to burn. It was destroyed by fire on three separate occasions. *Courtesy of KOP Shots.*

and metal fixtures, which were used to support the Confederate army. The church remained empty and abandoned through the war's end in 1865. In 1886, the church was once again, for the third time, destroyed by fire as another forest fire raged through the area. Several days later, almost as if to permanently solidify the destruction of the church, a great earthquake struck, inflicting even greater damage.

As Jacob Skelen discovered, very little remains of Biggin Church today except for a few walls…and the occasional ghostly encounter.

The Ghosts of Quenby Bridge

After being routed from what is now Moncks Corner, Lieutenant Colonel James Coates moved his Nineteenth Regiment of the British army to Biggin Church. With walls three feet thick, the church was nearly impregnable. This was mid-July, and the British leader had moved his men and supplies to the church as he retreated back toward British-occupied Charleston.

At about 3:00 a.m. on July 17, 1781, Lieutenant Colonel James Coates, realizing the difficult situation he was now placed in, burned most of the supplies and ammunition that he had stored in Biggin Church. Gathering his men, he proceeded across Wadboo Bridge on his way south. Before leaving the church, he left a note addressed to General Nathanael Greene along with some sick and wounded, asking that the invalids be treated with humanity and that they be sent to Charleston. He had thought that the colonial forces that were pursuing him were those of General Greene, but he was mistaken. He was actually being pursued by General Thomas Sumter, a young and arrogant leader nicknamed "the Gamecock."

Coates had three possible avenues of retreat: over Biggin Bridge down the west side of the Cooper River toward Goose Creek; over Wadboo Bridge down the east side of the Cooper River toward Strawberry Ferry; or again down the east side of the Cooper River but toward Quenby Bridge. With his Nineteenth Regiment he decided to march toward Quenby Bridge, yet he sent his cavalry toward Charleston through Strawberry Ferry near Childsbury.

Seeing Biggin Church burning in the distance Sumter roused his troops and went in pursuit of Coates, ordering his cavalry forces to race ahead of his infantry. In the rush to catch up with the British Nineteenth Regiment, Sumter left behind his six-pounder cannon, a decision he would regret later in the day.

Troops under the command of Colonel Peter Horry had been positioned at Wadboo Bridge to intercept the British but for unspecified reasons had deserted their posts. In regards to this matter, Lieutenant Colonel Henry Lee later wrote:

> *To our surprise and mortification, no opposition at the bridge* [Wadboo Bridge] *had taken place; and indeed our inquiries terminated in the conviction that the detachment destined to occupy the post* [Horry's] *had abandoned it a few hours after they had been sent to possess it. Hence arose our ignorance of Coates' movement, which could not have occurred had the militia party continued at their post, and to which ignorance the foe owed his escape.*

Colonel Lee and Colonel Wade Hampton gave chase, crossing over Wadboo Bridge, which had not been fully destroyed by Horry's men or had been repaired in the night by Coates's men. Now seeing that Coates had divided his forces, Colonel Wade Hampton rode in the direction of Strawberry Ferry. Yet by the time he reached there, the British captain in charge of the cavalry of the Nineteenth Regiment had already crossed. The ferryboats had been taken across and left on the opposite side.

Meanwhile, Colonel Lee's and Colonel Hezikiah Maham's cavalry, with General Francis Marion's infantry close behind them, followed Coates's trail in the direction of Quenby. Somewhere about a mile north of the bridge, they overtook Coates's rear guard under the command of Captain Colin Campbell. When Lee and Marion deployed against them, the inexperienced British troops attempted to prepare to receive them. When the order was given to fire, the recruits failed to discharge their muskets. Intimidated by the presence of the American cavalry, they panicked, and in a matter of minutes they surrendered upon being summoned to do so. About one hundred were taken prisoner along with supplies.

The colonial forces then continued their advance, and when Captain Armstrong of the Legion cavalry reached Quenby Bridge, he found that Coates's regiment had already crossed. Not certain whether he should continue over the bridge, which Coates's men had already begun dismantling,

Armstrong sent back to Lee asking whether he should attack, yet without mentioning that the bridge stood before him. Lee replied by messenger that the orders were to attack all before them. Armstrong galloped over the bridge with the first section of the Legion cavalry, with the second under Lieutenant George Carrington following behind, both knocking off some of the loosened planks of the bridge as they did so. Coates had prepared his cannon to receive them, but so sudden and unexpected was the charge that the men manning the gun, as well as the work party dismantling the bridge, fled before them. The rest of Coates's men—who were in a disorganized state, bottlenecked together in the causeway—were for quite some time helpless to organize to face the attack. Many fled.

Coates himself and a few of his officers became separated from their men and took a position behind some wagons, from which they traded saber thrusts with the Legion dragoons. The third section of Lee's cavalry, under Captain Ferdinand O'Neal, halted at Quenby Bridge. Maham and his cavalry then attempted to get over the now flimsy bridge to support Armstrong and Carrington, but having his horse shot out from under him, he and his men were stopped from proceeding. Captain James McCauley and some of Marion's infantry, however, were able to continue on and made it over to assist Armstrong's dragoons. Lee, now coming up from the rear, and Maham tried to repair the bridge, but with little success. In the meantime, Coates's men began forming up to counterattack. Armstrong, Carrington and McCauley, seeing themselves in risk of being surrounded, broke through the British ranks and made their escape through some woods. Moving down and circling around the end of the creek, they finally rejoined the rest of Lee's and Marion's forces, which were coming to approach Coates from that quarter. Lee marched the remainder of the cavalry up Quenby Creek, where Francis Marion joined him with his infantry and the Legion infantry. While this was happening, Coates had his cannon and his men withdraw to Shubrick Plantation (also known as Quenby Plantation) nearby, where they fortified themselves and awaited the American attack.

Lee and Marion, having crossed the stream, moved up through the woods and advanced to the edge of the open fields lying around the plantation. There they halted and surveyed Coates's position. The Shubricks' home was a two-story building situated on a rising ground, with numerous outbuildings, making it impregnable to cavalry and very formidable to infantry. Lee and Marion decided that it was too strong to attack. They then paused and awaited Sumter, who came up at about 3:00 p.m. Despite Lee and Marion's objections, and the fact that the artillery would be a long time in arriving,

Sumter decided to attack. At 4:00 p.m., the fighting began, with Sumter having deployed his men in the nearby slave buildings while putting his cavalry and the Legion infantry in the reserve.

Sumter then ordered up Colonel Thomas Taylor with forty-five men to take a strategically situated fence. During this assault, Major John Baxter was knocked from his horse by a musket ball. He shouted to Lieutenant Colonel Peter Horry, "I am wounded, colonel."

"Think no more of it, Baxter, but stand to your post," Horry replied.

"But I can't stand, I am wounded a second time!" shouted Baxter.

"Lie down then, Baxter, but quit not your post," responded Horry.

"They have shot me again, colonel, and if I stay any longer here, I shall be shot to pieces," Baxter said after being hit a third time.

"Be it so, Baxter, but stir not," Horry commanded. Baxter obeyed, but he was hit a fourth time. Fifty of General Marion's men were killed or wounded in this assault.

Taylor's men, moving up, came under heavy fire and were driven back by a bayonet charge led by Captain Skerett. Marion's musket and riflemen rushed up to aid Taylor and took position at the fence themselves, lying low on the ground for protection as they fired. There they remained, taking many casualties until, finally having run out of ammunition, they were forced to fall back. The battle having run for about two or three hours, Sumter withdrew back across Quenby Bridge (by this time repaired) and camped some three miles from Shubrick Plantation, after leaving the cavalry to collect the dead and wounded.

Singleton having the six-pounder cannon and more ammunition having arrived, Sumter had intended to resume the attack on the morrow but was met with the anger of his leaders. Colonel Thomas Taylor and his men were particularly angry at having been needlessly exposed to suffer so many losses, Marion's men feeling similarly. Colonel Taylor found General Sumter "sitting cooly under the shade of a tree." He said, "Sir, I don't know why you sent me forward on a forlorn hope, promising to sustain me and failed to do so, unless you designed to sacrifice me. I will never serve a single hour under you," and then retired from Brigadier General Sumter's command.

By the next day, inflamed with resentment at having been left exposed while Sumter's men were kept safely behind cover, all of Marion's men had gone home except for one company of about one hundred men.

Colonel Lee, also unhappy with how things had gone, buried his men in a mass grave near Quenby Creek and departed with his men to rejoin Greene's army in the High Hills of the Santee. After having the majority of his troops abandon him because of his arrogance and recklessness, Sumter decided not to continue the battle and the next day fell back across the Santee, having earlier arranged for boats for such a crossing. During the melee, he had managed to capture a British paymaster's chest with 720 guineas, which he divided among his own men. The entire battle lasted just three hours.

For many years afterward, it was said that the rains would wash up the bones of the dead and carry them out into the river. It is also said that the area surrounding Quenby Bridge is still haunted by the men and horses that died there. The sounds of battle can be heard throughout the night and into the early dawn. An apparition of a headless British soldier is said to be seen rushing the knoll toward the bridge to assist his long-dead comrades in a battle that ended more than 230 years ago, a battle that routed the British from their stronghold on Berkeley County in the war for this country's independence.

The Grave Robber and Benjamin Blackmon's Wife

This story is often erroneously attributed to Bamberg County, South Carolina, but the fact is that the people involved actually resided in Berkeley County. In fact, Benjamin Blackmon's last will and testament was filed in the Charleston District and noted that he had resided in St. James Parish and died at his Goose Creek plantation. Both St. James and Goose Creek are located in Berkeley County.

After the American Revolution, there was a period of severe economic instability. Many families left the upper section of the state and moved closer to the coast in order to seek a better living. The Blackmon family was one of them. In fact, Benjamin Blackmon became very wealthy.

Benjamin became infatuated with a young miss by the name of Mary Pye. They courted appropriately, and one day he presented her with a very large and beautiful diamond ring. The two were soon married, and Mary enjoyed her husband's success and wealth. Mary always wore the ring. Oh how she did love that ring. She showed it off to everyone, and soon everyone knew of the young bride and her large diamond ring.

As was often the case, an epidemic swept the area. Mary became very ill. Despite the best doctors' efforts, Mary continued to deteriorate. Soon she succumbed to the illness and fever that ravished her body.

The entire town knew of Mary, and everyone attended her funeral. One by one they filed by her open casket and paid their respects. The brokenhearted Benjamin Blackmon had his wife buried near their home. Even though she was dead, he could not bear to be separated from her. He had her buried in front of the plantation home. After the service he dismissed all but a few servants and went to his room to grieve his beloved Mary. He did not leave the room that evening and even refused dinner. The slaves were as heartbroken as he was, but they quickly became quite concerned that he would soon grieve himself to death. As they would check on him, they would hear him praying and begging God to return his beloved Mary. Eventually, the praying ceased, and the servants feared that he had died. One brave soul entered his master's room and found that he was indeed still alive but had apparently cried himself to sleep. Happy that their master was still alive yet saddened at his grief, the slaves eventually retired for the evening.

Late that night, they were awoken by a bloodcurdling scream. It was immediately followed by a far worse scream than anything any of them had ever heard in their lives. It was coming from outside the plantation house. Benjamin Blackmon grabbed his pistol and ran down the stairs to the door. As he threw the door open, there stood his beloved Mary. Her dress was covered in blood and dirt. She fell into his arms. In both horror and disbelief, he stared at his motionless wife lying in his arms. He then noticed that her beloved ring was missing…and so was her finger!

Once he convinced the slaves that Mary was not a ghost, he had them place her in bed and tend to her injured hand. He then had one of his servants leave to get the doctor. It was then that he went to investigate the grave site.

When he approached the grave, he found that it had been dug up and that a shovel was sticking out of the mound of dirt next to it. He cautiously approached the grave with his pistol in his hand. He held his lantern out over the hole, and there he saw a figure in the grave.

"Come up from there!" he shouted. The figure did not move. He again shouted, and still the figure refused to leave the grave.

Benjamin Blackmon took the shovel and threw it down on top of the figure in the grave. The figure did not move. Blackmon handed his pistol to a servant and carefully eased himself down into the grave opposite the seated figure. As he swung his lantern around to see the hooded face of the figure, he screamed at what he saw. The frightened servant also screamed and accidentally fired the pistol off, striking the wall of the grave and throwing dirt on both Benjamin Blackmon and the figure. Blackmon quickly told his servant that it was okay. He then stated, "He's already dead."

As Blackmon gathered his composure, he again turned the lantern toward the figure. It was that of an elderly man. In the man's right hand was a knife, and in his left hand was Mary's ring—and her finger. Once again he examined the face. It was frozen in a state of absolute fear. The sheer terror felt by the man was recorded in the man's last expression. It was such a grotesque distortion that Blackmon had to again look away. He left the man in the grave and returned home to Mary.

As authorities arrived the next day, they were able to piece together what had happened. Apparently, the man was a grave robber who knew of Mary and her beloved ring. He had apparently gone there to rob the grave and had cut the ring finger of the deceased woman—except that the woman was obviously not deceased. Apparently, she had slipped into a coma, and the attending physician had mistaken it for death. When the would-be grave robber cut off Mary's finger, the pain awakened her, and she let out a scream and grabbed the grave robber with her other hand. Obviously this action was not what the elderly grave robber had expected, and he responded with a scream of his own while simultaneously experiencing immediate heart failure.

In a further bit of irony, Benjamin Blackmon decided not to waste the grave. He had his servants refill the grave with the grave robber in it. He also had them use the dead man's own shovel.

Mary recovered from her ordeal. She eventually outlived her husband and even remarried, taking Frederick Schuler as her second husband. She eventually died—permanently—on July 4, 1860.

Medway Plantation

Medway Plantation always serves as a reminder to me of all the things that we take for granted in our youth. During the late 1970s, I was fortunate to be able to hunt the plantation and its adjacent properties. During those times, I met people and saw things that now, as an adult, I wish I had the ability to experience again. As a child, you tend to take for granted the once-in-a-lifetime encounters, and in fact it sometimes takes a lifetime to realize you actually had one. I encountered two living legends at the plantation and did not realize it until more than thirty years later.

My father once had business with Ray Walters, the caretaker of the property in those days, and he dropped me off at a wrought-iron gate in the company of an older black gentleman who was tasked with repairing the gate. Of course, I was rather miffed at not being allowed to accompany my father on "adult" business, and I was quite rude to the man with whom I was left. Regardless of my manners, he began to tell me tales of his work as a blacksmith. At the time, I did not realize that I was speaking with Philip Simmons, perhaps the greatest blacksmith and wrought-iron craftsman of Charleston. He began crafting horseshoes when he first started out, and by the time he passed away his work was considered more of an art form. His work can be found in the Smithsonian Museum, the South Carolina State Museum and even in France and China. He even received the Order of the Palmetto, which is the highest honor granted by the State of South Carolina. I really wished that I had paid more attention to the man.

Medway Plantation's builder never lived to fully enjoy his home. *Courtesy of Library of Congress Archives.*

Another time my father introduced me to the owner of the plantation. Her name was Gertrude Legendre. I politely shook her hand and did not realize I was meeting another legend.

Born in 1902, she was the daughter of New York carpet magnate and House of Representatives member John Sanford. Her grandfather, Stephen

Sanford, was a prominent businessman and chief executive officer of the Bigelow Sanford Carpet Company. Within this family, she became a socialite.

As a teenager, she begged her parents to let her go hunting after her graduation from high school. She much preferred this to becoming a debutante. Her parents granted her wish, and she killed her first elk in the Grand Tetons of Wyoming. She was hooked on big game hunting after that and eventually became involved in expeditions to exotic lands. In 1923, at the age of twenty-one, she began traveling the world as a big game hunter. It was on a safari expedition to Abyssinia in Africa for the American Museum of Natural History that she met her husband, Sidney Legendre. It was also on this expedition that she was almost killed.

At daybreak one morning, her guide spotted four lions, but as they approached, the lions started to move away. Gertrude Legendre fired once and struck a lion in the stomach and leg. The shot did not bring down the lion, and he managed to escape into the brush.

As they began tracking the injured animal, she caught another glimpse of him and managed to get off a second shot, only to see him vanish once again even deeper into the brush. They tracked him to a very dense, bushy area, where they heard him growling. They waited for about thirty minutes before the growling subsided. Figuring that the animal had succumbed to his wounds, they approached. They found where he had been lying soaked in blood, but the lion was nowhere to be found. They were now in the dense brush with a living lion—a very large, angry and injured lion.

As they huddled down in a tunnel created by a thorn bush, they heard a roar from about twenty feet away. The injured lion charged, and Gertrude's colleagues fired blindly at the beast. Another hunter within the group, O.M. Reese, wheeled around and fired both barrels of his Holland and Holland .470-caliber rifle. The lion skidded to within ten feet of the horrified group. They remained frozen in shock for several minutes before regaining their composure.

Gertrude Legendre continued as a big game hunter until 1929. She had many adventures hunting game and even had a standoff with a tiger that stalked her in her blind for fourteen hours before she was able to get a shot at him.

Gertrude spent many years being the hunter, but a series of events led to her being the hunted in 1944. She would find herself no longer the predator. This time, she was facing the rifle.

During World War II in 1942, Mrs. Legendre took a job in Washington managing the cable desk for the Communication Branch, which later evolved

One young woman is said to still be waiting for her husband to return from a hunt on Medway Plantation. *Courtesy of Library of Congress Archives.*

into the Office of Strategic Command (OSS). She handled sensitive and top secret documents for the division. By 1944, she was transferred to Paris and obtained the rank of second lieutenant in the Women's Army Corp. She also became a spy for the OSS.

On September 23, she was traveling through the western front in France with Major Max Papurt; Bob Jennings, an agent of the OSS; and their driver,

Private First Class Dick, in a jeep near enemy lines. Near Wallendorf, PFC Dick slowed the vehicle down, and a bullet struck the front fender. Major Papurt grabbed a rifle, jumped from the jeep and began attempting to locate the German sniper. The driver inched the vehicle along and had barely gotten ten yards when Legendre, Bob Jennings and the driver had to exit the jeep and use it for cover. With the next burst of gunfire, PFC Dick screamed out in agony and collapsed in the road beside the jeep. Legendre crawled to his side to tend his wounds. When she reached the injured soldier, she slowly and carefully peered up over the floorboard of the vehicle. Just as she did this, a round hit the front axle and ricocheted into the crankcase, spraying hot oil into her face. At that moment, Bob Jennings ran and grabbed Major Papurt, who had been pretending to be dead to avoid being shot again, and pulled him from the open roadway to cover behind the jeep. All four were now pinned down behind the vehicle, lying together in a mixture of slime, mud, blood and oil. Realizing that the situation was hopeless, Jennings tied a white handkerchief to the end of the major's rifle and hoisted it high above the jeep. In a few moments, the gunfire stopped. Bob Jennings and Gertrude Legendre quickly burned their OSS identification before they were swarmed by Nazi soldiers.

Gertrude Legendre and her colleagues were taken prisoner. She would spend six months as a prisoner of war, the first American woman to become one. Major Papurt would eventually die during an air raid while still in captivity. Bob Jennings was also imprisoned. PFC Dick was never seen again after being taken into captivity.

Mrs. Legendre was moved from location to location and was interrogated by the Gestapo but never revealed her assignment. Eventually, she was able to escape across the Swiss border with the help of a German lieutenant. After the war, she used her connections to find the German lieutenant and helped him and his family flee Germany and settle in America. I wish I knew then what I know now. I wish I had those opportunities again.

I have fond memories of the area, such as the time my father and I walked up on a "live" still. I mean an actual working moonshine still. As I recall, my father did not seem surprised, but nonetheless he ushered me out of the area. Some readers may be surprised at the fact that there was an active working still in Berkeley County in the 1970s. South Carolina just seems to hold on to its history and traditions—even the illegal ones. As a matter of fact, Spartanburg County sheriff's deputies made several arrests as recently as July 1, 2011, after they found a moonshine still, up to two thousand gallons of illegal liquor and $150,000 in cash. According to Spartanburg

Medway Plantation's architecture consisted of a stair-step roof, allowing evil spirits to step down and leave the house in peace. *Courtesy of Library of Congress Archives.*

County sheriff Chuck Wright, the arrests and seizure followed a ten-month undercover investigation of the operation in Landrum, South Carolina. As you can see, moonshine is still a profitable business in the state—until you get caught.

As a young boy, I also recall the plantation workers wanting to leave the plantation before dark. There was an obvious urgency in their desire that I noted even as a young boy. When I asked them why they had to leave, they told me of the ghosts of Medway. This time I listened.

Medway is the oldest house of record in the entire state of South Carolina. It was constructed in 1686. Charleston itself was founded in 1670, so the house is only sixteen years younger than Charleston. The house was built by Jan Van Arrsens for his wife, Sabina de Vignon. The Dutchman crafted the home in much the style of his homeland. When facing the house, one immediately notices the stair step–style gables. This was a Dutch design in architecture that combined design with superstition. The steps were designed in that manner to entice any evil spirits to walk down and leave the house in peace.

Unfortunately, Jan Van Arrsens did not live long enough to enjoy the home with his wife. Immediately after his death, she married Landgrave Thomas Smith, who was governor of South Carolina. Smith died at the age of forty-six, and his grave is marked by a marble stone on the property. There is no trace of a grave for Van Arrsens.

It is said that many who sleep in the upstairs bedroom on the south side of the residence awaken to the smell of pipe smoke. More than one guest has been startled to see Van Arrsens sitting in front of the fireplace, smoking his pipe and enjoying in death the home that he was deprived of in life.

Another "resident" of Medway can be found in the upper north room. Her name is Polly Seed. It seems that young Polly and Samuel Marion were very much in love. In fact, they were so much in love that they swore that even death could not separate them. They made a pact that whoever of the two should die first would meet the survivor in the upper north room.

One day, the inevitable came, and Samuel Marion passed away. As agreed on, Polly went to the room and waited. Her beloved never returned. Polly continued waiting and waiting until she herself passed on. It is said that she can still be seen waiting for her beloved Samuel.

Downstairs by the north window, the most pitiful of all the ghostly inhabitants of Medway can often be seen. For centuries hunts have been conducted on the plantation, where wildlife abounds. In earlier days, it was often a big event, with family and neighbors bringing their families together for the hunt and a celebratory dinner afterward. On one such occasion, a young newlywed couple was invited.

As the deer hunters prepared for the hunt, the young bride was overcome with a feeling of utter dread. She knew that if her husband attended the hunt, something horrible would happen. The feeling was overwhelming, and she begged and pleaded with him not to go. He just laughed at her and advised her that she was overreacting. He kissed her goodbye and ran off to meet his comrades for the hunt.

The young woman could not calm herself. No amount of coaxing or even teasing from the other wives could make her leave her post at the window. The day turned into evening and then the evening into night. Now the other wives also became concerned.

Eventually, the group of hunters returned. They were not laughing and happy as they usually were after the hunt. In fact they were the exact opposite.

The panicked young bride scanned the faces for her husband but could not find him. Then she saw the makeshift stretcher outside. Her husband had been mistaken for a deer and had been accidentally shot and killed. In one horrible act of mistaken identity, the happy young bride became a devastated young widow.

The family took her home and tried to console her, but eventually the woman grieved herself to death. At the moment, she was said to have returned to the spot by the window. Many claim to hear her dress rustling as she invisibly paces back and forth. Others claim to still see her by the window, where she continues to wait for her husband's return from a hunt that ended centuries ago.

The Old Goose Creek Church of St. James Parish

Charles Carrington had become bored with the party he was attending in Goose Creek and decided to go for an evening stroll. He found himself on the property of a very old church that at the time was surrounded by a large wall and an iron gate. As soon as he reached the gate, rain began to fall, and it forced him to run through the graveyard and seek shelter at the church.

As he sat at the church, waiting for the sudden shower to cease, he had an uneasy feeling that he was not alone. The feeling that something was not quite right overcame him. He then heard footsteps approaching, and he turned to see a young woman in the aisle. She knelt in prayer momentarily until she, too, realized that she was not alone. She introduced herself as Edith Coleman. She said that she was a member of an old Goose Creek family and that many of her ancestors were buried in the graveyard outside the little church in a family vault.

The feeling of dread left Charles Carrington as he gazed upon the face of the beautiful Edith. He was somewhat taken aback by the choice of conversation that she had decided to pursue. Edith spoke of death and of fear. She spoke of how foolish it was for people to fear death and the dead since it was a natural occurrence. In fact, wasn't death just another part of life? Surely, she said, the dead cannot harm the living, and in reality life is as great a mystery as death.

Carrington was not convinced by her reasoning. He feared the graves, the vaults, the graveyard and the heavy sense of a ghostly presence in the old

The Old Goose Creek Church is where Charles Carrington's dreams of love became a nightmare. *Courtesy of author.*

church. He could not wait to leave the structure. The rain eventually subsided, and Edith insisted on showing him the family vault in the graveyard. He did not want to go, but he humored the young lady. That was not all entirely true—he also went because he was quite charmed by the beautiful woman.

Eventually, Charles Carrington returned to the party. He asked about the old church and the beautiful young lady he met. The hostess interrupted and stated that he must have found St. James, the old Goose Creek Church. She stated that it dated back to about 1670. She also asked him if he had noticed the arms of England over the altar.

How could he not, he thought. He also had noticed the symbol over the front door. The damned ugly thing was huge. Big ugly bird feeding a lot of small ugly birds. The truth is, it frightened him. "The front door crest reminds me of vultures," he said out loud.

"The truth is the symbol was the marking of the Society for the Propagation of the Gospel in Foreign Parts, the society that had sent missionaries to found the church in Goose Creek. It symbolizes a pelican feeding her young by tearing flesh from her own breasts symbolizing the sacrificial acts of charity of the missionary society," he was told.

A pelican mutilating herself and forcing her offspring into cannibalism was not an image he wished to entertain. What a horrible symbol for a church, he thought. As a matter of fact, the thought of vultures and buzzards did not seem so bad to him now. If his friends were trying to make him feel better about the creepy old church, they were doing a horrible job. It definitely was not working.

No one seemed to know of the young Edith Coleman, but they did confirm that the Colemans were an old Goose Creek family.

During the next week, Carrington visited the church every evening to meet the lovely Miss Coleman. He pushed back his fear just to be with her. They would sit just inside the gates and talk well into the night. As could be expected, he began to fall in love with the beautiful woman.

On the other hand, Edith Coleman remained aloof at his interest in love. She spoke of love in such a serious manner that it concerned Carrington.

"Would our love outlive the fires of youth when the finger of time had placed its seal of age and decay? No, no, a thousand times no! Man's love droops, then fades, and dies," she declared.

The intensity of her words shocked Carrington, but he would not deny his feelings. "Put me to the test, Edith," he said as he reached for her hand.

Edith pulled her hand away before the young man could take it and laughed. She told him that he took such matters too lightly. Once again he told her to put him to the test.

"You swear it?" she asked.

"I swear it!" Charles Carrington insisted.

"Then follow me," Edith responded, and with that she got up and motioned him. He followed her from the gates through the cemetery to the family vault, where she ran ahead on that cool Saturday evening. She laughed and ran around the side toward the entrance. When Charles Carrington reached the vault, Edith was nowhere to be found. Bewildered, he looked at the door and wondered how she may have gotten inside to hide. He grabbed the iron handle and with all his might pulled until the door fell open. Something that had been lying against the inside of the door fell to his feet. As he looked, he could not believe his eyes at what lay before him.

It was the decomposing body of a woman in the tattered dress his lovely Edith had been wearing. In an instant, the realization of what he was seeing hit him. He released an ungodly moan and collapsed beside the corpse.

When people arrived for services the next morning, they found the unconscious Carrington beside the body of Edith Coleman. Edith had been

The crest that disturbed Charles Carrington. *Courtesy of Library of Congress Archives.*

the eldest daughter of James Coleman, had died many months before and had been placed in the vault. Further investigation revealed that the lid to Edith's casket had been removed and that the lining had been shredded by fingernails…from the inside. Obviously, Edith had not been dead. She apparently had been in a deathlike coma and had come out of it only to find herself trapped at the door of the crypt. Unable to escape, she died on her knees clawing at the door.

Charles Carrington physically recovered from his ordeal but was said to have gone insane from the ordeal. His mind was never able to reconcile his experience.

Another tale associated with the old church involves the burial of another young woman in the vault near the front door of the church. A young slave boy was tasked with bringing water to the church daily. He heard screams and cries from the vault but was so frightened that he was afraid to tell anyone of his experiences. When he finally refused to return to the church, he told his master of the "ghost." The master examined the vault and discovered that the young woman had also been entombed alive and had been unable to escape the vault. By the time the young slave had informed his master, it was too late.

The vault across from the front door is marked with a marble slab that reads:

Here lies the Body of
Elizabeth Ann Smith
The Amiable and Deservedly Beloved Wife of
Captain Benjamin Smith
Who died the 26 March 1769
Aged 27 years
Also Their Daughter
Mary Smith
Who Died September 9th 1768 Aged 3 Years 5ms. and 8 Days

During those times, epidemics spread rapidly, and their causes were not understood. When a person died of a disease, there was a rush to bury them for fear that the disease would leave the deceased body and look for a new living host. People were often rushed to burial and oftentimes were not dead. They would be in a comatose state that would be mistaken for death by an attending physician in his haste to prevent further infection of a community.

CAPTAIN "MAD ARCHIE" CAMPBELL'S WAGER

Captain Archie Campbell was quite an arrogant and prideful man. As a member of the king's army, he was entitled to wear the white breeches and gold braided red coat that signified him as a British soldier. The problem with Archie was that he prided himself too well. He was rude, arrogant and boastful. In fact, he was described as a "wee bit of a smug bastard" by his closest friends.

Captain Campbell was quite smitten with the beautiful young Paulina Phelps. He liked the sweet and innocent Paulina. She was not demanding like other women he had known. He liked the fact that she was quiet and timid. He wanted a wife to look up to him and admire and adore him as much as he adored himself. He wanted a wife who worshiped him, a wife he could control. Paulina was just such a woman, he thought. He just did not understand why she pretended to have no interest in him. Yes indeed, he absolutely was a smug bastard.

The bells of St. Michael's church rang as he hurried along Meeting Street to his destination. The windows were filled with lights just as the air was filled with the sounds of music, laughter and merriment. Captain Campbell had arrived. Now the party could begin. He strode up the steps and handed his cockaded tricorn hat to the butler. He then went into the drawing room to bow low over the hand of Mrs. Tidyman, the hostess.

The year was 1780, and Captain Campbell found many friends there at the social gathering. Charles Towne was occupied by Royalists and Loyalists alike. Those in attendance who were not British were surely Tory allies.

One person who was not in attendance downstairs was the lovely Pauline. Captain Campbell continued through the building, through the hall and up the stairs to the ballroom above. He stopped momentarily as his eye caught the one thing that could slow his search for Pauline: a mirror.

After pausing to admire his reflection, he continued into the ballroom. Immediately he found her, her white gown billowing about as she danced. She tossed her hair back and laughed. She was quite a beautiful sight in her expensive gown and her dazzling jewels. Wealth had a tendency to make women even more attractive to Captain Campbell.

The captain frowned when he saw the flirtatious glances that Pauline was giving the young soldier who was her dance partner. When the dance was over, he strode over and bowed to claim the pleasure of the next dance. She informed him that it was already taken. The gentleman smiled with a smug satisfaction that rivaled even that of Captain Campbell himself.

Campbell watched as his rage mounted. "Who is this young puppy?" he asked of his friends.

"He is the new lieutenant from Philadelphia," was the response. "Challenge him for his arrogance."

"Never mind," said the captain. "I intend to marry the lady."

A burst of laughter from his companions caused him to raise his voice. "I will indeed challenge him, but first I shall be married."

"Married?" their eyes turned to the beautiful Pauline, who was gazing at the young lieutenant. "It looks as if the wedding will not be yours!" they teased.

"Gentlemen, do you honestly believe that this young popinjay could win her from me?" responded the captain.

"I'll wager," began one of his friends, but the captain cut him off in mid-sentence.

"Nay gentlemen, it is I who will wager. I will wager my Arab filly to fifty pound of yours. I wager that in three days I will be married to that lady."

The others scoffed at the idea, to which the captain added, "with her consent."

"Taken, taken," laughed the men as all shook hands. They thought it was a shame that he should lose the lady and even worse that he should lose a fine horse.

The next day, Captain Campbell drove up to the door of 43 East Battery. He had come to take Pauline, "Miss Polly" as she liked to be called, for a ride in his carriage behind a very spirited steed. Miss Phelps had sent back a response to his request that she would be pleased to go. She could not resist

Mad Archie Campbell recited his vows with a pistol pointed at the preacher and another at the bride. *Courtesy of Library of Congress Archives.*

a ride through town in such a wonderful carriage. She would be noticed and envied by all of the ladies since she had not one but two British suitors. She donned her blue cloak and her prettiest bonnet with the brightest plumes. She allowed the captain to assist her into the high seat.

He drove the horse quickly. Soon they had left Charles Towne behind in a cloud of dust and were in the country. He struck the horse with the carriage whip, and the horse responded by rearing and then bolting wildly. Again and again he struck the horse, encouraging it to go faster and faster. The horse raced madly over the rough road, slinging mud. Faster and faster he drove the horse as he ignored Pauline's pleas to slow down.

"Ah, Miss Polly. It is so lovely to see your eyes so large and your lips are so red, and my steed does love to run. He will not listen to reason. Reason, Miss Polly? Who cares for reason? It is glorious to ride with you, like flying, Miss Polly, my sweet. Let us fly together to the skies!"

"But Captain Campbell, I…"

"No 'buts' my lovely. On and on we go to the road that has no turning," the captain responded.

On and on they went until they had reached the Goose Creek Church. Captain Campbell pulled up to the door of the rectory, and Mr. Ellington came out. Paulina, half fainting, was helped from the carriage. When she recovered, the captain insisted that they had come to be married.

"Not without the consent of the lady," responded the parson.

The captain then drew his pistol and pointed it at the man. "Unless you comply, you shall be instantly shot, and the lady's virtue could only suffer in consequence. I say, Sir, make haste!" He then produced a second pistol, which he placed against Pauline's head. He smiled a smile of sheer madness. "The lady does consent. Do you not, my dear?"

"Yes, oh yes!" she responded wisely. They were then married there at the church, just the couple, the preacher and two matching pistols. Afterward, they returned to Charles Towne.

Pauline told her family of the tale and the marriage. She said that it was not until they arrived at the church and the captain had explained his intentions that she ever thought of seriously marrying him. She would later say that even had he not had a pistol to her head she would have married him anyway after that exhilarating ride to the church.

Captain Campbell won his lady, fifty pounds and the nickname "Mad Archie." His happiness was short-lived, for he was captured at the Battle of Videau's Bridge in 1782 as the British made a raid to capture slaves and steal them and supplies from the colonists. He attempted to escape and was shot dead by Nicholas Venning. Pauline died a few months later while giving birth to their only child.

The couple had spent their short time together at Exeter Plantation in Moncks Corner. The plantation was destroyed by fire in 1967, and Berkeley Country Club now occupies the ground were it once stood. They say that you can often hear Pauline crying for the child she left behind as she walks along the large oak trees at the entrance to the country club. It is also said that you can also hear the laughter of Mad Archie Campbell in the old St. James Church in Goose Creek and see him standing in the doorway in his bright red coat with a pistol in each hand.

Hangman's Tree

About ten and a half miles from the Berkeley County line, crossing into Georgetown County, there stands a cypress tree along St. Delight's Road. It is an odd-looking tree with a nasty scar on the side facing the highway. This side, at one time, had a very large branch that stretched over the highway until a tractor trailer rig with an exceptionally tall load struck it several years ago and it had to be removed. This old tree is easily identifiable since it is the only tree along the roadway that has been barricaded by the highway department with protective steel railing barricades. Perhaps this was done in order to protect it from damage should some weary driver fall asleep and travel over in its direction. Then again, perhaps the two counties decided that enough people had already lost their lives on this tree over the past few centuries. This tree is known as Hangman's Tree.

Although it is located in what is now Georgetown County, it was once part of Berkeley County and was used as a place for execution for criminals, unruly slaves, nonpatriots and anyone else who was "deserving" to be made a public example. The corpse would be left hanging in the tree dangling over the highway as a deterrent to anyone who may have a notion to violate the laws of the land as they were passing through. There was nothing more rehabilitating to a would-be criminal than traveling under that massive limb and watching the crows and buzzards feasting on former ne'er-do-wells. Even after the electric chair took over as South Carolina's favorite form of capital punishment and hangings were stopped, the tree still stood tall as a reminder to those entering or leaving Berkeley County that nonsense was

Hangman's Tree once served both Berkeley and Georgetown Counties. Its usage dates back to the Revolutionary War. *Courtesy of KOP Shots.*

dealt with swiftly. Even as a small child, I recall traveling under that massive limb as we traveled to my grandmother's home in Myrtle Beach. I also remember my mother often accelerating just a little as we passed it. Maybe it was a child's imagination or maybe it was real, but that tree always seemed to bother us just a little.

Once, as we passed under the tree, I saw a man sitting on the limb. He waved as we passed by. No one seemed to notice the man but me. Even when I said something, my siblings never saw him, and my mom shushed me about it. Again maybe it was an overactive imagination, perhaps someone was hiding in the tree or perhaps there was something paranormal at play. I don't really know which, but one thing is for certain: I have never liked that damn tree.

Hangman's Tree got its start in the days of colonial South Carolina. During the American Revolution, there were those who opposed British rule and those who were still loyal to the king (Loyalists or Tories).

After the fall of Charleston to the British, colonial forces near Moncks Corner learned that a group of Tories along with a few British forces were headed for the town of Pineville. The colonial forces sent out a scout named Joe Edie to warn Francis Marion, who was resting in the area. Marion was an elusive leader of the colonial forces known as the "Swamp Fox" because of his ability to fight and then completely disappear into the swamps and forests of Berkeley County. In fact, one British officer, Lord Charles Cornwallis, referred to the swamp in which he was chasing Marion as "one hell of a hole." This area of the swamp is now known as Hell Hole Swamp.

Edie warned Francis Marion and then warned all the people in the area to bury their valuables and hide their supplies. They were also told to hide their livestock deep in the swamps. He also carried a message to the men to meet Marion the next morning in a specially designated spot deep in the Santee Swamp.

Tories were plentiful in the area, so Francis Marion wrote a letter to a friend and Patriot stating that he and his men were in Jamestown resting. He sent forth the letter knowing that it would be captured by Tories and that the information would be used by opposing forces to capture or kill him and his men. It also would divert the opposing forces from Pineville.

Joe Edie alerted Captain Bonneau, who got his things in order, buried his valuables and went to meet Marion. The group of colonists then intercepted the opposing force, killing several and taking numerous prisoners. The rest of the Tories fled back toward Moncks Corner.

Among the prisoners was a man who identified himself as "Jack Sprat." This was more than likely a name he gave his captors during interrogation in order to prevent them from identifying his family and other Loyalists. He obviously took the name from the nursery rhyme that became popular after its publication in 1765 in *Mother Goose's Melody*. Regardless, it did not help the Loyalist. In fact, he had been captured riding one of Captain Bonneau's horses and had in his saddlebags some of the possessions Bonneau had buried on his property.

Since Jack Sprat insisted on protecting his companions, he was seen as having a code of honor and his loyalty was rewarded by Captain Bonneau. Bonneau's men prepared a rope and gave it to the prisoner, with the orders for "Jack Sprat" to hang himself from a large cypress tree. Much to the colonists' surprise, the man did just that. He climbed up in the tree, secured the rope to the limb, placed the noose around his neck, smiled and waved to his captors; then he leapt to his death. As a deterrent, his body was left hanging from the tree, and in fact it is said that his bones hung there for many years after his death.

It is said that Jack Sprat haunted the tree for many years and could be seen sitting on the branch up until it was removed. Perhaps this is who I saw in the tree as a young boy. We will never know because Jack Sprat disappeared when the hanging branch was removed.

Another story associated with the tree concerns another Tory, by the name of Dave Peigler. He and his brother, Dan, were notorious Loyalists. Dave was a tavern keeper and was suspected of being involved in the murders of several colonists, although there was no proof other than he would end up being in possession of the horses they were last seen riding. He often threatened to capture one of the leaders, Captain Theus, and have him hanged. There was no love lost between Theus and the Peigler brothers.

Sometime in 1779, information was received by Francis Marion that a group of British forces was moving into the area. Captain Theus was a member of Marion's forces, and he and a scouting party were sent out for reconnaissance. The captain's plantation was located along the path the party took, so they stopped there to replenish supplies. They quickly learned that the Peigler brothers had raided it just a few hours before their arrival. They had driven off the horses and cattle and had boasted that they had ran the rebel forces out of the area. They then told the frightened slaves that they would return and burn the house to the ground.

Of course, this did not make Captain Theus very happy. He had all but one of his men leave and retreat to a previously designated rendezvous location. As was customary in those days, rebel colonists would have their most trusted slaves hide in the woods near their plantations and keep watch to alert them of danger. Captain Theus did this, and then he and his companion tied their horses in a secluded garden and went inside to have dinner. As they sat down, one of the slaves burst into the home and advised them that one of the Peigler brothers was galloping up the road alone.

Dave Peigler reached the house and was swearing and cursing. He said that he had left one of his pistols in the dining room and that he would cut the throat of every negro in the place, take what he wanted as payment for having to return and then burn the entire place to the ground. It would have been very easy to shoot him as he stood in the yard cursing and securing his horse. In fact, the one colonist raised his weapon to do so but was stopped by Captain Theus. Theus drew his sword and stepped behind the half-opened front door. The other colonist caught the idea, stepped behind a hall door and removed a buckskin cord. Dave Peigler walked through the door with pistol in hand. In the next instant, Captain Theus struck him with the butt of the sword with such force that the blade broke at the hilt. As Peigler hit the floor, both men pounced on him and quickly secured his hands with the cord. Even then, Peigler continued to resist until he felt the cold muzzle of a pistol in his ear.

All bravado left Peigler in an instant. He began begging for his life. Captain Theus ignored him and walked out the front door, where he sounded his horn. Instantly, a grinning servant appeared with a rope and tied Peigler's feet. He then took the pistol and kept guard as Captain Theus and the other colonist returned to their dinner. Neither ever spoke a word to Peigler.

Having heard the horn, Theus's men returned to the plantation. They took control of the prisoner and placed him on a horse. They also placed the rope that had secured his feet on the same horse. They had coiled it up very nicely and secured it behind the prisoner.

As they rode away from the plantation, Peigler thought long and hard about the rope and his fate. He decided that it was better to be shot or stabbed through with a saber than to be hanged. As they traveled along, he decided to take his chances. He leapt from the horse and ran into the woods, his hands still secured with the buckskin cord.

"Take him alive!" shouted Captain Theus, and the men began to circle the area into which he had ran. Peigler might have actually been successful in his escape had he not caught his foot in some vines and fallen. He could do very little to free himself since his hands were tied behind his back. He was soon recaptured and dragged back to the road. The captain began to inspect the trees and located a sturdy cypress. There were very little formalities; the rope was introduced to the tree and the prisoner was introduced to the rope. The colonists removed the saddle from the horse and placed Dave Peigler on it. They placed the rope around his neck, and as they were making final adjustments, they noticed a cloud of dust about a quarter mile up the road. As the men watched, they noticed the sun reflecting off the metal equipment and realized that this was a British unit heading in their direction. Captain Theus quickly cut a switch and struck the horse on which Peigler sat. The startled creature darted off into the woods, leaving Peigler twisting and turning at the end of the rope. All of the colonists mounted their horses and fled into the woods, leaving Peigler dangling from the limb.

It was not long after that Captain Theus's slaves and others began to report they had seen the ghost of Dave Peigler sitting on the church steps in St. Stephen's churchyard. He was said to have a rope around his neck, a bottle of rum in one hand and a pistol in the other. He was seen both night and day, and the slaves reported that he looked as real as he did when he was living.

Eventually the war ended. Dave's brother, Dan Peigler, had met his death during a horse race in which he fell and broke his neck. This occurred on his wedding day. When he did not show up, the wedding party waited for three hours. Eventually, they received word of his death. One man in the crowd, a friend of both the bride and groom, offered himself as a substitute for the recently deceased. Apparently, he was a lot closer to the bride because she readily accepted and they were married. Everyone was quite happy that day and even happier when they got rip-roaring drunk after Dan Peigler's funeral the next day.

About ten years after Dave Peigler's hanging, Captain Theus entered Boinest's Tavern while on a trip. As he entered, he was astonished to see the late Dave Peigler tending bar. Captain Theus walked up and asked the man, "Are you not the Dave Peigler whom I hanged ten years ago?" He noted that he was and then told him that had the British been more interested in Theus and his crew things might have been different. He said that it took a lot of rubbing and a pint of liquor to bring him back around. He said that the British captured Joe Edie, one of Theus's men, and hanged him with the same rope with which Peigler had been hanged (ironically Joe Edie was the man who saved Francis Marion and caused Jack Sprat to be hanged in that same tree in the previous story). With that, Dave Peigler stated, "I reckon, Captain, that clears the score between us, and you and I mays well be friends." Peigler then poured the astonished captain a drink. The captain paid for his drink and never returned to the bar again.

Hangman's Tree had many more victims over the centuries. Many of the condemned are alleged to still haunt the tree. It is also said that at times even the long-removed branch returns. The phantom limb can be seen stretching over the roadway as if it has returned to await the arrival of its next victim.

Hags, Hants, Boo-Daddies and Root Magic

As stated in the earlier tale concerning the town of Childsbury, the slave population brought with it its own culture and folklore, which eventually combined with the others in Berkeley County. The slaves formed what would be known as the Gullah or Geechee culture of the Lowcountry of South Carolina and the state of Georgia. With the culture came its own group of spirits, demons, ghouls and magic, as well as a vast array of entities and an equally vast array of methods to deal with them. Some entities were mere nuisances, while others could be quite deadly. The latter usually required the help of a conjurer or root doctor to assist the victims in ridding themselves of the entity. Root magic was, and still is, considered to be a very powerful form of magic throughout the Lowcountry.

In the Gullah culture, there were the simple ghosts known as "hants" or "haints." They were the ghosts of deceased people who refused to move on. They were considered nuisance spirits and were said to be more prevalent at the time of a new moon.

"Hags" were a little more dangerous. They would creep up on you while you slept and ride you like a horse. The victim would be unable to move, and sometimes the hag would beat the victim and suck the life from them as it rode them. Oftentimes a conjurer had to be called in to catch the hag. The hag catcher consisted of a mason jar filled with pins and needles. The conjurer would sit in the room with the sleeping victim, and upon seeing the first signs of trouble he would grasp the jar and wave the trap above the victim while speaking a conjuring spell. The hag would be captured

The slaves who were brought to the area also brought with them their own skills, beliefs and customs. *Courtesy of Library of Congress Archives.*

in the jar, and the jar would then be sealed and buried. Hags could be demonic entities, but they could also be the spirits of the living. The spirits of the living that intended to do harm to the victim often left the evildoer at night while they slept and inflicted harm on the victim as he or she slept. These spirits were known as "boo-daddies." When a boo-daddie of a living owner was captured in a hag trap and buried, the owner would inevitably suffer a very painful and horrific death due to the fact their soul had been trapped in a jar and buried, and they would be forced to sit on pins and needles for eternity.

"Plat-eyes" were shape-shifters and could turn themselves into any form. They were often witches or conjurers, and similar beings—such as the Cherokee witch Spear Finger—can be found in Native American folklore.

"Money lights" were named after the light that the slave Money carried through Childsbury. These lights or balls of flame are also known as "jack-o-lantern lights" and also "spook lights." The slave Money had created this light as a means to frighten off those curious about his comings and goings. You will soon learn about a few such lights that were not man-made and about those who encountered them.

"Drolls" were the spirits of children who had died painful deaths. They were also the spirits of children who had drowned in the swamps and could be heard crying at night in the marshlands. The children were often the victims of the Cymbees, a race of spiritual entities that resided in the pools and marshes of the Lowcountry. The Cymbees would often entice unruly children to the edge of the water and then drag them in and drown them.

In the St. John's Parish of Berkeley County, the Cymbees were believed to dwell in the limestone sinkholes that were once predominant in the area. This area consisted of what is now Santee State Park, Lake Moultrie, Lake Marion and the Santee Canal.

In 1860, Henry Ravenel published an essay entitled "The Limestone Springs of St. John's Berkeley." He visited the springs on the majority of the plantations that have since been destroyed and are now covered by the waters of Lake Moultrie. Another source of information regarding the

A spring similar to those believed by the slaves to be inhabited by the Cymbee. *Courtesy of author.*

Pooshee Plantation was said to harbor a Cymbee in its spring. *Courtesy of Library of Congress Archives.*

limestone springs of the area comes from the documentation of the travels of Edmund Ruffin.

On March 25, 1843, Ruffin documented that he had visited Woodboo Plantation. It was there where he first noticed the limestone springs that he referred to as fountains. It was at the plantation that he first heard about the belief among the slaves regarding the Cymbees. Every fountain of any considerable size was said to be inhabited by one of these spirits. Each fountain was different, and each had a different and unique Cymbee. A slave driver who accompanied Ruffin said that he had never seen the Woodboo Cymbee but had been told that it was web-footed like a goose. An elderly slave had also told him that he had never seen the Woodboo Cymbee but had seen another at a different fountain. He said that he had seen the Cymbee sitting on a plank that had been laid across the water. She had long brown hair that hung down and covered her face, body and limbs. After seeing her, she glided off the plank and disappeared into the water. The old man had seen her when he was a youth and admitted that he had been quite frightened by the encounter.

At nearby Pooshee Plantation, Ruffin heard the tale of a young slave boy who had encountered a Cymbee there. The creature was running around and around the fountain. He learned that the Cymbees were usually seen at night and were usually found sitting on a low bridge or plank crossing the water. They also could be found on the edge of the steepest side of the water. Ruffin noted that sometimes the fountains stopped and dried up and that new ones took its place. The slaves explained this as the Cymbee dying or having been offended and having moved on elsewhere. When the Ravenels enclosed the fountain at Pooshee Plantation, the slaves protested in fear of offending the Cymbee.

In documents belonging to Henry Ravenel, he states that the Cymbees were often described as part human female and part fish, much like a mermaid. He also concluded that the word "Cymbee" was of African origin.

In a paper presented at the 2000 fall meeting of the Southeastern Regional Seminar in African Studies, historian Ras Michael Brown agreed with Ravenel's conclusion as to the word's origin. Brown contended that "West-Central African nature deities, called *simbi* spirits in Kikongo, served the enslaved people of the early Lowcountry as spiritual benefactors around which captives of diverse African origins and those born in the Low country built their communities."

Brown specifically pointed to a Kongo proverb: "Where your ancestors do not live, you cannot build your house." He went on to argue that nature spirits allowed those who were either strangers to the area or lacked ties with named ancestors to "still have access to the agents of Other Worldly powers and to feel attached to the land where they lived." Brown stated he believes that "cymbee" was an attempt to represent the pronunciation of the Kikongo word *simbi*. The words match in not only their sound but also their meaning. He further stated that nature spirits known as the *bisimbi* (plural of *simbi*) often take the form of water spirits, and he believed that the Lowcountry example is unmistakably derived from West-Central African understanding of *simbi* spirits.

Many rituals of these beliefs involved making sacrifices of some sort or another. Fruit would often be offered to appease angry spirits. Often sacrifices such as these were placed in the Colonoware pottery created by the slaves. The sacrifices and the pottery would then be cast into the waters of these springs, ponds and rivers to satisfy the spirits. Fragments of such pottery and sometimes even whole artifacts can often be located on dives in these waters.

As a young jailer in Berkeley County during 1985, I was introduced to the "root magic" of the local culture. Root magic is a conglomeration of many beliefs, including that of Haitian voodoo, African hoodoo and Native American witchcraft. I would often search incoming prisoners and find small bags containing sticks, bones, rocks and other assorted paraphernalia. The prisoners would become upset and tell me that I was basically contaminating their magic. I was informed that the bag was a talisman prepared by a root doctor to protect its owner from harm. I cannot attest to its effectiveness based on the fact that it did not prevent the owner from being incarcerated, but I can tell you that the owners believed in their power and that one had better respect their beliefs.

My very first encounter with root magic involved a man who refused to remove a small quantity of Spanish moss from his ears. That's right—the man had stuffed Spanish moss into his ears. He advised us that he had been told to do so by a conjurer. The root doctor had told him that this would keep evil spirits from whispering in his ears and telling him to do bad things. I do not know if the man suffered from a medical condition that created the delusions of voices in his head or if a hant or boo-daddie was actually communicating with him. It did not matter. One thing I did realize was the fact that the man believed so strongly in the root magic that he was willing to fight to keep the moss from being removed from his ears. The head jailer, an older black gentleman from the area, knew far more about root magic than I did and asked the man if he could examine

Above: The author covered in duckweed while investigating a spring similar to those believed to be inhabited by Cymbees. *Courtesy of Swamp Fox Diving.*

Below: Piece of Colonoware pottery located underwater by the author during a dive in Berkeley County. *Courtesy of Swamp Fox Diving.*

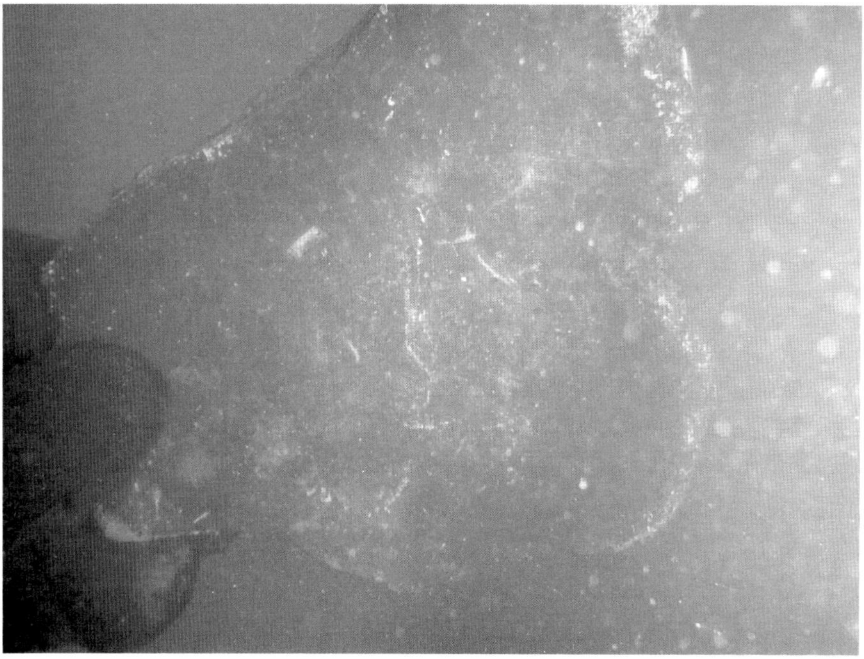

the conjurer's work because he had experienced the same issue with evil spirits. The ruse worked, and the old man examined the homemade fungal earplugs. Satisfied that they were not illegal or dangerous contraband by any means, the wise jailer allowed the man to keep them in place and thus avoided a violent confrontation for all of us. As he explained to me, "The spirits may or may not exist and may or may not hurt you. I will take my chance with the spirits. A man who believes in the spirits and is afraid will kill you. Never take a chance with a man like that."

DICKEY WANTS A RIDE

Legend has it that the British officer, Lord Charles Cornwallis referred to the swamps between Berkeley and Georgetown Counties as a "a hell of a hole" in a letter written to King George. It was the hiding place of the Swamp Fox, Francis Marion, during the American Revolutionary War. He was said to have known those swamps like the back of his hand. As a rebelling colonist leading troops against the Crown, it paid to know the area inside and out. He would strike and then escape into the cover of dense swamp and the national forest that now bears his name.

Others also used the swamp as an escape. Runaway slaves and chain gang prisoners often fled to the swamp to escape pursuers. Bootleggers during the days of prohibition also sought refuge in those swamps. They made their corn whiskey known as moonshine there, hid it there and often fled from the law into that very swamp. In fact, notorious gangster Al Capone was said to have had relatives in the area, and the Hell Hole Swamp area may have been one of the biggest, if not the biggest, suppliers of illegal liquor to the Chicago area and the entire country in those days.

As you can imagine, with gangsters came violence. The headline in the local paper read, "Murder and Mayhem in Moncks Corner," after a shootout between rivals left three men dead in the area. In fact, in just a short period between May 19 and July 24 in 1930, there was so much violence that the area earned the nickname "Bloody Berkeley." On May 19, one man was killed and another wounded; on May 31, a man was shot on his doorstep; on June 3, a man was fortunate to survive being shot at; and on July 24, a man was gunned down on Main Street in Moncks Corner.

According to local author William Schuler, "In the old days in Berkeley County, you did one of two things: you worked on a farm or you made corn whiskey." My grandfather grew up during that time, and he was a farmer—I think.

My uncle Thomas and my mother use to tell me a tale regarding my grandfather and the swamps between Georgetown County and Berkeley County known as Hell Hole Swamp. It seems that quite a number of the folks who escaped into the swamp never came out. If the gangsters did not get you, then the gators, snakes and swamp bogs would. Bogs are like quicksand, only nastier. Maybe the Cymbees might get you, or maybe old lady Spear Finger (a later chapter) might get you. Right now, let's focus on my grandpa and the night he met "Dickey."

In those days, most common folk traveled by horse or mule. If you went to work, you often went in a group in a wagon pulled by some worn-out four-legged creature such as a horse or mule. I do know that there were even carts made for children that were pulled by goats. People were quite creative in those days.

One night, my grandfather was traveling with a group of men through the swamps. Darkness had crept up on the weary "farmers" and caught them by surprise. The last thing any of them wanted was to be in that swamp after dark. There were things in that swamp that came out after dark that no one wanted to encounter. There were gators, snakes, bear and an assortment of wildcats of all shapes and sizes. There were also *other things.*

Along their path was a rather long and narrow wooden bridge that covered one of the nasty little aforementioned bogs. All of the men had heard stories of things attacking people as they crossed this bridge at night. Anyone of those men would have given everything they owned to be anywhere other than where they were that very moment. As they were approaching the bridge, the men grew more and more apprehensive. Whether it was the horse sensing the men's fear and apprehension or something else, it chose to stop dead in its tracks as it rounded the corner and saw the bridge. Its ears moved forward and its mane stood on end as if electrified. The men felt something, too.

The driver urged the horse forward, but the most he could get was a few steps forward and a few steps back. This little dance was repeated several times, which only increased the men's anxiety. They were getting nowhere fast, and it was only getting darker in the swamp. They did not want to chance losing what little moonlight they had.

The driver advised the men to sit tight and hang on. He was going to get the wagon across the bridge, but first he had to do some *negotiating* with the horse. He got down off the wagon, very cautiously went to the edge of the road and cut a long switch from a nearby tree. He then returned and climbed back into the wagon. He took off his hat, placed it under his rear and sat down on it. He then turned his attention to the horse and urged it forward.

Again it only took a few steps. Then he hit it with the switch. The horse bolted forward as if it had been bitten by a snake. It headed straight for the bridge. As soon as the horse reached the bridge, there was a loud cry from the woods beside the bog; "Dickey wants a ride!" it shrieked.

The horse snorted in fear as it hit the bridge. Immediately a large ball of fire flew up from the bog. As soon as the horse's hoof touched the first wooden plank of the bridge, the ball of fire flew up on to the bridge and into the back of the wagon. It landed directly across from my grandfather. "Dickey wants a ride!" it shrieked again and again.

The men wanted to leap from the wagon, but there was nowhere to go. They were in the middle of the bridge with the bog on each side with a shrieking ball of fire sitting next to them. "Dickey wants a ride!" it continued to shriek.

The horse burst into an all-out run for its life. What was actually mere minutes seemed like an eternity to the men, but the end of the bridge was drawing closer. As soon as the horse's hoof struck dirt, the ball of fire flew up into the air and out of the wagon. As it departed it screamed, "Dickey wants a ride, and Dickey got a ride too!" and it laughed maniacally—"hee, hee, hee, hee!"—as it flew back into the swamp and disappeared.

My granddaddy's story was retold by my grandma, my uncle and my momma for years, and it was always one of my favorites growing up. They told how granddaddy explained that the ball of fire, as he described it, was bright and intense but gave off no heat. I used to laugh at the thought of a ball of light sitting across from my granddaddy and what old Daniel Roberts must have been thinking. I used to think it was funny until I found out firsthand what he probably felt as I ran through the woods on the other end of Berkeley County one night many years later.

Sheep Island Road and the Summerville Light

Ever since man invented the train, there has always been a connection between railroad accidents, disasters and the paranormal. Often a location of such a disaster will develop a paranormal phenomenon. These oddities can manifest themselves in the form of balls of light and are referred to as "spook lights," or simply "lights."

The lights appear in locations such as Paulding, Michigan; Surrency, Georgia; Gurdon, Arkansas; and Wilmington, North Carolina, to name just a few. In fact, President Grover Cleveland had an encounter with the Wilmington light in 1894 while traveling by presidential train. This light is commonly known as the Maco Light and is named after the station where it is located. It is said to have come into existence after the tragic death of a conductor named Joe Baldwin in 1867.

Summerville, South Carolina, has its own spook light. Between Highway 17A and Highway 176 is what remains of a cut-through road known as Sheep Island Road. It is also unofficially known as Summerville Light Road, or simply Light Road. This road, or the nearly five-mile-long dirt section of it, is the location of Summerville's most famous—or infamous—ghost tale.

In the 1800s, Sheep Island Road was not a deserted dirt road but rather an area where train tracks existed and ran into the growing town of Summerville. One of the local train's conductors had a very faithful wife who would meet him in that area every night. She would stand beside the tracks, lantern in hand, and wait for the train's approach. Upon seeing the

Sheep Island Road, the location of the Summerville Light. *Courtesy of KOP Shots.*

lantern, the train would make a special stop just to let him off to join her. The couple would then walk home arm in arm every night.

One night, the train ran behind schedule. The anxious wife waited and waited, and as more time passed, she grew greatly concerned. Finally, she saw the light of the train in the distance. She raised her lantern high and frantically swung it back and forth. The train finally slowed to a stop, and she ran to the engine. The engineer had a somber look on his face beneath the lantern's glow. As the other workers gathered around, they informed her that there had been an accident. Her husband had lost his grip, slipped from the train and had been run over. The wife screamed in horror and disbelief and demanded to see the body. The workers had to physically restrain her as the emotional engineer advised her that it would be best if she did not. He told her that when her husband fell under the train, he had been decapitated by the wheels. The wife screamed at the horrifying news and fainted. Some crew members remained with her as the train continued into town. A wagon was sent back, and the traumatized woman was placed in the back and transported home. Once there, she had to be carried inside. Friends and family could do very little to console the poor widow. The town physician and even the couple's pastor were unable to help the grieving woman.

The wife never recovered from the shock and never came to grips with the harsh reality that her husband was not coming home. Eventually, she began to take her lantern and walk along the tracks every night to greet her husband. Initially, the train would stop out of courtesy and compassion, but eventually it became too painful for the crew to have to convince her every night that her husband was dead.

After a while, the train would just pass her and continue on into Summerville as she frantically waved her lantern for it to stop.

Eventually, the old widow died, but her dedication and love for her husband never ceased. Oftentimes, the train would see the light, only to get close enough to realize that no on was there. Eventually, the train stopped traveling the tracks and they were removed, but the conductor's wife's nightly visits continue to this day. You can still see the light from her lantern as she walks the road where the tracks once ran, waiting for her husband's return.

Many folks claim to have encountered the eerie lights of Sheep Island Road, including Sandra Baxley, a local reporter who documented her experience in the *News and Courier* in 1970. The light sent her and her traveling companion into hysterics before it disappeared. Many others have reported their encounters in local newspapers for decades, and still others have taken to the Internet to tell of their experiences. Some claim that the light has produced dents and scratches on their vehicles, while others claim that their vehicles stall. Some have reported interference with electrical equipment, causing malfunctions, while others claim that the light causes metal objects to heat up to an uncomfortable temperature, including jewelry and even the rivets on jeans.

This area, now blocked off from travel and posted with "no trespass" signs, was once a favorite parking spot for young men to take their dates for a little secluded romance. More often than not, the young couples encountered more than they had bargained for. Many a car from many eras has raced along that road to escape the light. In fact, I know of one young rookie deputy in the early 1980s who had an encounter with the light and left the area very quickly—backward.

In 1986, I was a young deputy fresh out of the academy and eager to save the world. I was assigned to the South District of Berkeley County, an area that included Sheep Island Road.

One squad meeting, our sergeant, Johnny Richardson, was giving assignments. As we were departing for our 11:00 p.m. to 7:00 a.m. shift, Johnny stopped me and told me that I needed to patrol back along Sheep Island Road because the sheriff's office had been getting complaints of teens partying in the area. He further advised me not to stay too long in one area, not to flash any lights and not to go too far down the dusty old dirt road because I would not be able to turn around if the light chased me.

"Light?" I asked.

"Don't tell me you have never heard of the Summerville Light," he responded. I have heard of many tales, but frankly, that bit of Lowcountry lore was not one filed away in my cranial library. He proceeded to tell me the story I have just retold.

After preliminary preparation for a long night shift, I gassed up the old Ford Crown Victoria cruiser and headed out. I made my nightly stop at the convenience store and grabbed a cup of coffee (no doughnut) and headed for Sheep Island Road. The road has a long paved portion that passes over Interstate 26. There were concerns that the partying would get too carried away and that the participants would decide to start throwing objects off the overpass and down on the interstate for fun.

I patrolled along the paved portion as instructed. Johnny had told me to not, under any circumstances, go too far beyond the pavement or flash my headlights. He said that a favorite trick of the locals was to flash the headlights three times off and on, wait a few seconds and then flash them again. Then they would turn the car around and wait.

"Why?" I asked.

"When the light comes, it comes slowly, but the closer it gets, the faster it gets. When it gets close, folks take off and run like hell in their cars. That's why you turn around. If you don't, she will get you."

I just laughed, but now I found myself at the end of the pavement. My front wheels dropped off onto the dirt. Very slowly, my back tires did the same. I slowly crept a few hundred yards down the road and put the car in park. Can you guess what the young deputy in his starched uniform and shiny new badge did? Yep, I turned off my lights. Then I turned them on again. Then back off. Then back on. Back off—wait—back on and then off.

I had done everything Sarge had told me not to do, except turn my car around. Sure enough, a red light began to glow down the road. As it got closer, it seemed to move faster. It turned white. I laughed and slowly opened my door. I knew beyond a doubt that Johnny was trying to scare me. He had told me the story, left way ahead of me and waited on me to show up. He knew I was a rookie, and he knew how I would react. All he had to do was wait on the flashing headlights, spook me with his flashlight and watch me run off in a hurry. He and the rest of the squad would have a good laugh at my expense.

"Not tonight, Sarge," I mumbled under my breath.

I figured that the red light I initially saw was Johnny stepping on his brakes as he exited his cruiser. I also imagined that the white light that was now coming toward me was the light from his big metal Mag-Light flashlight. As the light approached, I quietly slipped out of my cruiser. As a safety feature, our interior lights had been disabled to allow such tactical deployment. It was designed to keep us from being illuminated as we got out of our vehicles on calls. At this point, I was more concerned with not being caught by another good guy than I was being shot by a bad guy. I slipped quietly around the rear of the car and over to the shoulder. I then crossed the ditch and began to walk slowly toward the light in a flanking maneuver. I had planned to pass the light, come in behind Johnny and use my own flashlight to scare him. I would be between Johnny and his car, and when he saw my light and panicked, Sarge would have to flee Light Road on foot. I was going to use my sergeant's own joke against him! I snickered to myself at my ingenious plan.

Unfortunately, it did not work. As I approached the light, I came to within about three car lengths directly parallel to it. I immediately realized that there was nothing holding the light! It was now an eerie greenish color, and it illuminated the road in a green haze. Johnny was not there. No one was there. As I felt my knees get weak, the light immediately shot straight up about forty feet in the air and flew off into the woods. The smart rookie had outsmarted himself.

I screamed like a schoolgirl, turned, started to run and fell face first in the ditch. In a move that would have made any action hero envious, I continued moving forward on all fours and then pushed myself up to two feet and made it to the cruiser. As I cranked it up, I realized that Johnny had been right, not only about the light but also about the inability to turn around. I backed out as quickly as I could. I was so thankful that the academy had taught me how to back up rapidly and for long distances. As soon as I hit the pavement, I spun the car around, threw it in drive and was out of there!

I went straight home. I had to change uniforms before I got a call and someone saw me in the shape I was in. As I walked in, my wife asked me what happened. After I used the house phone to let dispatch know where I was going to be for about twenty minutes, I told her. She laughed and said I was crazy. She did not believe me, and at that point, I was not sure I believed myself. I jumped in the shower and washed off the large portion of Sheep Island Road that I had brought home with me. I swapped uniforms and cleaned the mud out of the car while waiting on calls. I never told anyone on that shift what had happened.

Back home, the disbelief continued. That weekend, I took my wife's brother, who was in the U.S. Navy, and a friend, who was in the Coast Guard, out to Sheep Island Road. Both did not believe me. I did the same thing, just as Johnny told me, and once again I deliberately did not turn around. Sure enough, the light came so close that it lit the interior of the car green. It was the size of a basketball and hung suspended in midair. As I listened to two grown men whimper, I was glad that the seats in the cruiser were vinyl, and I prayed that none of us would inadvertently test their waterproof capabilities. The light stopped about a car's length away and burst into several hundred firefly-sized lights that then dissipated. We all started breathing again and went home. I never doubted Johnny ever again, and those two never doubted me again.

Many years later, I was a lot less frightened of things. Twenty years of law enforcement makes you a little less jumpy. By this time, I had retired from law enforcement. I missed investigations and doing research, so I joined a Summerville-based paranormal group and started doing some research for them.

I learned that Sheep Island Road had not been a passenger train line, as the group had been told. It had, however, been a tramline, and the tram was used in logging operations to haul felled trees into Summerville for use in creating lumber to build the town. In fact, the area is owned by Westvaco Forestry, and its offices are located a few miles down Highway 17A adjacent to a subdivision called Tramway (another indicator that the information was correct). I was not able to document any deaths along the tramline, but that does not mean there were none.

One thing of extreme interest to the group that I did find involved signal lanterns. I learned that the signal used at that time to make a train move forward was to swing a lantern up and down in an arc. A person would swing the lantern out straight directly in front of him up to his shoulders and back down to his knees. From a distance, this looks like a white light flashing off and on—just like headlights flashing. I also learned that red lanterns were used to make trains stop, and green lanterns were used to advise a train to travel slowly. All three of the colors have been attributed to the Summerville Light. I saw all three colors on the two nights as it approached me.

The group planned an investigation of Sheep Island Road, and I went with it for a rematch with the light. In order to keep vehicles off the road, the entrance had been blocked by a mound of dirt. Farther down, the road was impassable by vehicle due to large amounts of water. We all entered on foot.

Pretty soon, a light began to glow at the end of the road. Cameras began flashing, and videos were started. I spoke up and said, "Who is going down the road to see what it is?" I got no response. "Who is going with me?" Finally, I got three volunteers: my friend Alessa, a kid on crutches and an old lady half dead with emphysema. We started out together, but I am the only one who completed the five-mile trek there and the five miles back. When I reported that it was headlights, I was met with snarls and growls. I had debunked their hunt.

At the next meeting, I was preoccupied and did not attend. In my absence, I was voted out of the group. They were extremely upset that I had debunked their investigation while still maintaining my own claims of a past encounter. A friend who was in attendance told me that there had been an equal mixture of jealousy and fury. I received an e-mail advising me of the members' decision and instructing me not to come back. I still laugh about that to this day.

It is amazing how twenty years in the field of law enforcement had changed the rookie from an easily frightened Barney Fife to a seasoned and cynical Dirty Harry who would walk the entire length of the road and back, in the dark, armed only with a flashlight and a cellphone. I also know that what I encountered back in 1986 was not what I encountered with that group. I cannot say that what I encountered on Sheep Island Road in the '80s was the ghost of the conductor's wife, but it was definitely something that I cannot explain more than twenty-five years later.

And yes, I definitely understood what my grandfather felt with his encounter with a "spook light" decades before I was even born.

The Nazareth Cemetery and Headless Annie

Another interesting ghost tale from the Pinopolis area is that of Headless Annie. Just outside the gates at the Wampee Plantation entrance lies a little cemetery called the Old Nazareth Cemetery. According to one account, this is the home of that restless spirit. I was recently informed of this story by the father of someone very close to me, and as many times as I have been by that cemetery, I had never heard the story before.

It seems that many years ago, Miss Annie was the wife of a very abusive man. He used to beat Annie unmercifully, and in fact, one night he actually came home in a drunken rage and accused her of cheating on him. Annie was supposedly a very beautiful woman, and to ensure that no one would ever be able to gaze upon her beautiful face again, he cut off Annie's head. He then hid her head and it was never found. The man was charged with her murder, and Annie's body was laid to rest in the cemetery…minus her head.

According to legend, Headless Annie is trapped between life and death in the cemetery and is wandering for eternity, searching for the head her husband removed. The man never revealed where he hid it, and no one has ever found it—including Annie.

The man who told me this story says that this was a popular legend in Pinopolis back in his younger days. Many folks would try to prove their bravery by staying the night in the old cemetery outside Wampee, and he was included among the ranks of those who would defy Headless Annie.

One night, his father left him and some friends there at the cemetery. Home was in walking distance, and everyone knew one another in the area

Left: The Old Nazareth Cemetery. *Courtesy of KOP Shots.*

Below: Headless Annie is said to haunt the cemetery at night. *Courtesy of KOP Shots.*

back then. Nowadays you have to be more concerned about what the *living* people can do to you. There are plenty of evil ones around who are still breathing, but back then they were more concerned with what the dead might do to you if they got their hands on you.

The young man was in his early teens, as were his comrades. They were full of themselves, as most young men are, and of course were trying to top one another's "what if Annie comes" strategies. After all, how much trouble could a headless ghost be? She couldn't see you to chase you.

The boys had been dropped off outside the cemetery, and after working up their courage, they went inside it. Not long after they got inside, the trees began to sway back and forth, and the wind began to howl as if a storm was on its way. The boys began to look around for some shelter, and that's when they noticed something very peculiar about the wind and the approaching storm: it was only happening *inside* the cemetery. Everything on the outside of the little graveyard was perfectly still. Not a single tree was swaying. Not even the moss hanging from the old live oaks was moving.

The youngsters decided that if this was what was happening before the sun went down, they did not want to take any chances on what might happen after sunset. According to the storyteller, they opted not to meet Headless Annie that night and hurried out of the cemetery and back home before she made her presence known.

THE PLANTATION HOUSE AT WAMPEE

The grounds of Wampee Plantation and the house itself are considered by many to be the most haunted places in Berkeley County. As the previous story indicated, you have to first get past the cemetery and Headless Annie to even get into the gates leading up to Wampee. Once inside the gates and outside of Annie's reach, there are even more restless spirits walking the plantation grounds.

Many Native American tribes inhabited Berkeley County. The Cherokees were quite predominant, but there were many more tribes, such as the Etiwans and the Wassamasaws. Even today there is a section of Berkeley County known as Varner Town that includes descendants of the Etiwan, Catawba, Edisto and Cherokee tribes. The town is located near Carnes Crossroads, near the city of Goose Creek. Several Indian Schools were established in the community, including the Varner Indian School, established in 1939 and closed in 1963. The Varner Town Indians are all that remain of what was a vast and diversified Native American culture that covered the county. There were at least twenty-five different tribes identified by the colonists starting with the letter "W" alone, such as the Wando, Wantoot, Wappaoola, Westo, Wisboo and Woosah, just to name a few of them. These tribes, like countless others across North America, were uprooted and moved by colonization. Such is the case with the Wampee House.

In 1696, Baptists established Wampee Plantation in St. John's Parish. Several houses were erected on the property, and the current house was the third in the series. It was built about 1822, when the plantation was

Wampee House before restoration. *Courtesy of Library of Congress Archives.*

Wampee House as it appears today after extensive restoration by Santee Cooper. *Courtesy of KOP Shots.*

prospering through the cultivation of rice. The property was owned by Charles Macbeth, who happened to be the mayor of Charleston during the Civil War. The current house is much smaller than most of the plantations of St. John's Parish due to damage from a tornado during its construction. As the house was being framed, the tornado struck and broke off the framing at the sills. This forced the builders to saw off the broken timbers and build the house much smaller than originally planned.

In 1939, several Indian burial mounds were discovered on the Wampee Plantation grounds. The burial mounds, or tumuli as they are called, contained evidence that indicated that the occupants interred there more than likely had been killed in battle with early colonists in the area. According to accounts, the positioning of the bones indicated violent trauma. There were both male and female bones located. These are believed to be members of the Etiwan tribe. In 1955, a member of the excavation party, William "Bill" Wiley, wrote a paper entitled, "Tumuli in the Pinopolis Reservoir." In his paper he eloquently reminded us of the injustice done to the Native Americans at Wampee.

> [T]*he Etiwans evidently continued their retreat westward and established a new frontier across the Wassamassaw, which goes beyond the confines of the Pinopolis reservoir (Lake Moultrie). Eventually the Etiwans, as well as practically all other Indian tribes in the low country, were driven out or exterminated. We in America who now condemn aggressor nations across the sea should remember that our forbears also were aggressors when they ruthlessly drove out and destroyed this native people. What a pity there is no one left among the race of Hiawatha, and no hand to lay a wreath upon these graves. There is no indication that there will ever be erected a shaft perpetuating the memory of the Etiwans who fought and died to save their own homeland.*

The Etiwan Indians in these mounds apparently died defending their homeland against the colonists whom they saw as intruders. Legend has it that in one of these tumuli a young Indian woman was found in a crouching position. She apparently died in battle, as did her male counterparts. She died defending her homeland, a place she did not want to leave. And she didn't.

According to legend, a young Indian maiden can be seen wandering about the Wampee House and the grounds surrounding it. This began immediately after her burial mound was disturbed by the excavation performed by the archaeologists. Unlike the stereotypical imagery Hollywood has placed in our minds, she is not dressed in deerskin and buffalo hides. She is dressed in flowing blue robe and slipper-like footwear. The robe is said to resemble silk chiffon. The blue is said to resemble the blue water hyacinth flower that grows in marshy areas near Lake Moultrie. It is also called the Wampee Flower. The young maiden is also said to have a complexion like a porcelain doll.

For many years, Wampee House stood abandoned and desolate. It's windows were shattered, and the house stood seemingly in ruins. In his book *Plantations, Pineland Villages, Pinopolis and Its People*, Dr. Norman Sinkler Walsh stated that during his childhood and early teen years he found the Wampee House "a somewhat dangerous place to explore." He went on to describe his last adventure there as a child:

> *I was not aware of any ghost stories about Wampee when I was growing up in Pinopolis. This changed, though, when I was twelve years old. On one exploratory visit with my friends, I led the way onto the porch and opened the door. I was amazed to see a woman's figure on the stairway landing, between the first and second floors. The figure stood near a window on the stair landing. She had a pale, indistinct face and was wearing a transparent, chiffon-like flowing garment. I don't remember being afraid; however my friends and I left in a hurry, and I never went back.*

Others have also encountered the "Blue Maiden." The location has since been restored by Santee Cooper, a water and electric utility company. Lake Moultrie was built on the majority of the plantation grounds along with several other former plantations. In April 1934, the governor of South Carolina signed the bill to create the South Carolina Service Authority commonly known as Santee Cooper. The project created two lakes, Moultrie and Marion. It took more than two years to complete. In order to build the lakes to create the power, more than twenty historic plantations were destroyed.

Santee Cooper acquired Wampee by eminent domain. Basically the state needed the property and seized it without owner's consent in order to use it for the betterment of the state by creating a public utility. The owners at that time, the Cain family, were extremely upset that they were forced to surrender the property. The Cain family filed a lawsuit against Santee Cooper stating that Wampee Plantation was not critical to the construction of the hydroelectric plant. In 1945, the South Carolina Supreme Court agreed with the Cain family and returned Wampee to them. Santee Cooper was determined to have the property and made a very lucrative offer to the Cain family, far greater than the $12.19 per acre others had received. The Cain family accepted. Wampee was the only surviving plantation house of the project, and Santee Cooper renovated the house for use as lodging for visiting dignitaries and for business meetings.

More than 177,000 acres of land were appropriated requiring Santee Cooper to obtain the titles to 1,326 tracts of land. The result today is that Santee Cooper provides power to 1.7 million South Carolinians.

Since restoration, many have stayed in the Wampee House and had run-ins with the apparition. A former caretaker encountered her as she was putting away dishes. She noticed a figure outside the window, and when she looked out, she observed a clear image of a young Indian woman standing on the front porch. The Indian maiden was staring straight at her and vanished right before her eyes.

Rachel Bayless Smith is the granddaughter of one of the former caretakers. She grew up hearing the adults talking in hushed tones about unusual occurrences in the old house. She did not put much stock in the legend until one evening when she was walking by the house. As she passed, she got an uneasy feeling that she was being watched. As she stopped in front of the house, she looked up and saw a woman in a flowing blue gown looking at her through a second-floor window. The woman simply faded into thin air as if she had evaporated.

When researching this story, my daughter and I went to the location to take some photographs. Neither of us encountered the Blue Maiden, but we did encounter one of Santee Cooper's security officers. The gentleman advised us that he has not seen the Blue Maiden but did admit that the grounds get very interesting after dark. He stated that although he did not see the young Indian woman, he did have an encounter with another apparition on the grounds. While patrolling the area in the wee hours of the morning, he was surprised to see what he believed was a Native American on horseback near one of the gates. The figure simply guided his pony to the edge of the woods and vanished. He said that he never would have believed anyone else telling him the story had he not experienced it himself.

Several people have experienced other phenomena in the house. Ms. Smith stated that one night, when her grandfather was caretaker, a severe thunderstorm rose up on the lake. As the storm raged on, there was a knock on the door to the caretaker's house. He answered it to find three men completely drenched. When he invited them in, they told him that they had been out on the lake and had been surprised by the sudden storm. They said that they had been having difficulty finding their way to shore in the dark until he saw the lights of the first house and used them as a guide. They said that they arrived at the house and beat on the door, but no one answered. The three men then walked to the second house and knocked until their host answered. Ms. Smith's grandfather was astonished and said that the first house was Wampee House and that no one lived there. In fact, he had turned out all of the lights hours before, and there was no one there to turn them on. He was just as equally shocked when he observed the lights on in the locked house when he investigated after the storm.

Many believe that this incident was caused by a second spirit inhabiting Wampee House. This apparition is believed to be that of a pirate who wandered off while unloading a ship at nearby Stony Landing. It is believed that he died lost and wandering in the woods trying to find his way back.

Many report hearing doors open and close inside the house. Some Santee Cooper board members can attest to that. In a 1997 article in the area newspaper, the *Post and Courier*, Santee Cooper board member Mac Walters described his experiences in the house one night:

> *He awoke in the middle of the night and felt a presence that forced him to keep his eyes closed. His body was straight and his hands were clasped across his torso in a funeral fashion. He could not move. The sounds of doors opening was interrupted by an alarm at 4:30am. It was set for 6:30am. He never went back to sleep and heard doors opening the rest of the night…Five weeks later, he wrote about his stay at Wampee. Saying he still had not gotten over that night and would resign from Santee Cooper's board if he had to stay there again.*

A similar incident was relayed by the current caretaker, Sandy Gibson, to reporter Dan Brown of the *Berkeley Independent* newspaper. This involved two individuals who, one would believe, would not be easily frightened. Mr. Gibson states that in about 2000, Santee Cooper was shooting a promotional video and had former Super Bowl legend Terry Bradshaw and Detroit Lions center Steve Mott staying at the house as guests. He says that Bradshaw called him at about 10:00 p.m. or 11:00 p.m. that night and told him that Mott refused to stay in the room and was scared to death. Gibson asked what they saw, and Bradshaw told him to just come and get them. Gibson said that he arrived to find Mott shaking like a leaf and packing his clothes. Gibson said he told Bradshaw that he would put Mott up in a hotel, and

Coffins and their occupants being prepared for relocation and reburial. *Courtesy of Library of Congress Archives.*

One of the six thousand individuals whose graves where removed and relocated. *Courtesy of Library of Congress Archives.*

then Bradshaw also started packing, stating, "You don't expect me to stay here by myself, do you?" Wampee House managed to frighten a four-time Super Bowl winner away. Perhaps he encountered the disembodied head floating above him, as a visiting New York businessman claimed happen to him one night. Whatever it was the two NFL players encountered, they never revealed it.

One last incident occurred many years back on the same grounds. The same young man who had been searching thc graveyard for Headless Annie in the earlier story was forced to ride through Wampee one night on his ten-speed bicycle. As he was peddling through, something stepped out of the bushes behind him. He stated that he heard it begin moving toward him, and as it ran he began to hear claws striking the path. Adrenaline kicked in, and he began peddling faster, especially when he realized that the creature was bipedal—it had two legs and claws, not four. The young man said that he never looked back and kept peddling for home, with the creature chasing him. He stated that he turned into his drive, leapt off the bicycle and ran up the stairs and through the front door before his bike ever stopped rolling. He was inside with the door locked before the bike ever hit the ground.

He never found out what was chasing him and said that he never wants to know. Perhaps it was just a young man's overactive imagination on a dark, starless night, or perhaps it was one of the long-dead Etiwan Indians shape-shifting into something a little more sinister as he continues in death to protect the lands that were once his in life.

What makes Wampee Plantation the most haunted place in Berkeley County? Perhaps the fact that it is the only survivor in the Pinipolis area of a long-passed era that makes it that way. Or perhaps a contributing factor is the desecration of a few Indian graves.

If the graves are the issue, take into consideration that during the Santee Cooper Project, more than ninety-three cemeteries were relocated. That means that more than *six thousand* graves were disturbed. The individuals were dug up, removed and then reburied elsewhere. Without modern equipment such as ground-penetrating radar, it is quite certain that many were left behind to be covered by the lakes. This is what former state senator James Hammond believed and documented in several narrative poems in 1961. Likewise, Native Americans believe that the desecration of a grave is a sacrilegious action and disturbs the eternal rest of the one interred. In some belief systems, it forces the spirit to return and wander the earth eternally. Such may be the case with the Blue Maiden at Wampee. If true, then she is not alone. There are about six thousand others wandering the area with her.

KECLEH—KUDLEH

THE CHEROKEES' HAIRY SAVAGE

As stated in the previous story, Native American tribes once flourished in Berkeley County. Their history, tales and legends have long been lost to time due to the simple fact that they were spoken and not written. Spoken stories tend to eventually fade into obscurity. Written stories last for posterity.

We are fortunate that in 1821 a Cherokee silversmith named Sequoyah created a Cherokee syllabary, allowing the Cherokee people to read and write their own language. This was the first time in recorded history that a member of an illiterate people independently created a writing system. This allowed the Cherokee people to save their legends and stories in written form so that future generations knew them as their ancestors did. The fact is that by creating a writing system, Sequoyah actually saved Cherokee folklore.

The Cherokee people believed in many different entities, from gods and immortal beings to the Little People that lived in the forest. The Little People were similar to European leprechauns or fairies. They were about knee high and had long hair that dragged the ground, like with trolls. They could be mischievous, but they also liked children and helped them find their way home if they became lost. If treated respectfully, the Little People and the Cherokee coexisted well. If they were slighted and treated disrespectfully, they could be very dangerous and could bring illness and even death to those who offended them.

Another hairy, but much taller, creature that the Cherokees were familiar with was called Kecleh-Kudleh, which translates into "hairy savage." He

Many Native American tribes, such as the Cherokees, were once indigenous to Berkeley County. *Courtesy of Library of Congress Archives.*

was a very large creature completely covered with hair. He also had an awful smell. His stench often preceded him.

As the name indicates, he was not very friendly at all, and the Cherokees gave Kecleh-Kudleh a wide berth. Most people refer to the hairy savage by another name taken from a Native American tribe from Canada. That name roughly translates to "wild man of the woods." It is a derivative of the Salishan language of the Halkomelem tribe of southwest British Columbia. That word is "Sasquatch."

Regardless if you call him Kecleh-Kudleh, Sasquatch, Bigfoot or even Skunk-ape, apparently he still resides in Francis Marion National Forest and Santee Swamp, according to some. In fact, several individuals have filed their encounters with the Bigfoot Field Researchers Organization, a scientific research group dedicated to the investigation of these creatures. The following descriptions of encounters within Berkeley County were taken directly from the statements of the witnesses. The following are their own words taken from BFRO reports:

> *July 1993—First of all I don't believe in Sasquatches. Second I don't care if you believe me or not (Nobody does, except the person that was with me).*
>
> *As a boy I just about lived on the Banks of the Santee, every summer my Grandparents would camp on the Santee River. My granddad would take me out of school on the last day of the school year, and we would go straight to the Santee River and just about stay all summer. My Granddad use to tell us stories of a bear or something that look like one, my grand-mom would make him stop because it would scare me so.*
>
> *She just would tell me he's trying to scare me so I didn't ever believe him until one hot summer night about 18 years later a group of friends wanted to go camping but wanted to go somewhere real secluded. Since I was always in the woods they asked if I knew of any place. I told them that I did know of a place on the Santee River about a mile from the Dam. The next thing I know plans were set to go. A girlfriend of mine at that time wanted to go also so I gave everyone directions on how to get there and my girlfriend and I would set up a day early and see them the next day there. I haven't been to this place since my Granddad passed away, it was too hard on me to go back but I felt like I was ready to try it again 10 or so years later.*
>
> *The Santee lake and around it is swampy and the lake is full of stumps and a lot of moss in the trees. It a very beautiful place to go, but not too many people go to the river side of the Dam. The river starting from the Dam is 51 miles from the ocean. I know this because my mother caught a flounder there and someone took a picture of it and put it in the paper. They told the story of it and that it was 51 miles from the Ocean. I know all about that river and I know where the great Swamp Fox* [Francis Marion] *is buried way back on the river also. Anyway, my girlfriend and*

I got to Wilson's Landing about 3:00 PM on a Friday, that's a bait shop just behind the Dam, from there the paved road turns into dirt and mud. We drove about a mile back into the woods along the river to a place we used to camp. Nothing has changed one bit except for the trash on the river.

The river is at some spots about 200 yard wide and 1 foot deep. In some places it is only 20 feet wide and 15 feet or so deep. When the water comes out of the dam it is split into by an island. I have never been on that Island because it is very swampy and full of snakes. My uncle still hunts on it though. As a matter of fact this is why I'm telling this, he has heard something there and doesn't know what it is so I told him my story and he is the only person who didn't laugh. You name it, it's on that island: snakes, wild hogs, deer, lots of deer, people say they seen bear and gators. I am now saying there is something that walks on two legs and is not a bear.

As I was saying we drove way back there and started to set up camp. To our right there is a cleft about 50 ft high with bushes and what not on it. You know I'm not going to make a big story out of this, I'm just going to tell you what happened. We're in the woods, it's dark and we hear things on the river. My girlfriend (who was new to this camping thing) kept asking me, "What was that," on every little thing. That was an owl, that's a frog, that's deer jumping into the river from the Island.

"Are you sure someone isn't down there throwing bricks in the water?" I told her it would have to be cement block to make that loud of a sound. But I will take the light and shine down to the river and look. I went over to the edge and shined all around and didn't see anything. The noise stopped also. So everything is fine for about thirty minutes. Then I mean deer were jumping in that river like crazy. I have to admit, and it could have been her asking all those questions, I was getting a little nervous.

Then it happened; SOMETHING was coming up that cleft and I mean it was breaking branches and you could hear the dirt falling down from the weight of it. There is no way a deer can climb that bank. It was getting closer and closer and it didn't take but one "what?," out of her to get me in the truck looking for my gun. I couldn't find it and I was yelling out to her asking where is my gun, she answered "I don't know," from the passenger seat, "...but here's the keys let's go." I jumped in and fired up the truck and started driving out praying I wouldn't get stuck, not here, not now. We made it to the dirt road and I hung a right, we left everything at camp, food, tent, lantern burning, and somewhere my gun! I have never been that scared in my life! I must have drove 50 feet and then I slammed on the brakes and yanked her left and stop facing the way we were leaving. "What are you doing?," she asked. "I grew up in these woods on this river and I am going to find out what's back there." She didn't say a word. I started off and was going about 2 mph and looking with my high beams on. I was looking for something, deer or bear or something.

We started around the curve to the left. Just around the curve is the drive to camp, I don't want to go there, so I told her we would drive up a little past camp and turn around. I didn't go maybe 5 or 10 feet past the drive when this thing stepped out in front of us. I hit the brakes! "What is it?" she asked. "I don't know let me back up so I can see." All I saw at first and SHE SAW was two long hairy legs, I started backing up so my lights would spot it better since it was too close to the truck.

GOD as my witness and hers, this was no bear, this thing was maybe 7 or 8 feet tall and big, hairy and wet, it didn't stand real straight like you and me would but more at a slump from the waist up. It had the reddest eyes I have ever seen, and it just looked at us, frozen, looking, not moving at all, just standing there. "OH my GOD! My granddad was telling the truth after all." Then it just looked to his left and leaned as his leg started to turn, then he moved the other taking about a three foot stride, until it was out of site, gone into the woods. This thing walked on two feet and was not a bear.

Hello? I live in South Carolina! I said earlier that I don't believe in Sasquatches but how am I to explain what we saw? One night that changed me and her forever. The next day we saw those foot prints and they were bigger than mine, I saw the cleft and all the broken branches and the dirt that was dug out from it. Nobody will believe me when I tell this story but that's ok I don't care, I know what I saw and that's that. This was 7 years ago and the only reason I'm thinking about it now is because of my uncle who was telling me something last night. Something he heard in the swamp/woods on the Island of the Santee River.

There is one thing, but it could be just the area. We smelt an awful smell. Like dead fish or animal. It could have been just a change in the wind from the river. A lot of times when the river drops fish get stuck in the pools on the rocks. The water dries out and the fish die and stink. I don't think much of it. I couldn't smell anything on the road with it standing in front of me because the windows were up.

May 2002—I think I might have seen something while I was in South Carolina last May, but I'm really not sure. Anyways, I live in Florida and last May I went on a Herping trip to South Carolina looking for snakes to collect and photograph. While I was in Francis Marion National Forest walking a trail with my eyes set to the ground on the side of the trail looking for snakes I saw something leap across the trail about 50 yards ahead of me from left to right in one leap. It was on two legs about the size of a person or bigger and was uniform brown in color. This is basically all I saw. I was only about 15–20 minutes into the trail when this occurred. The trail was very narrow but straight and densely wooded on either side. I was by myself and I never saw anybody else on the trail or in the park during my time there. I know this is disjointed but let me try to describe this further. After I saw this thing leap across the trail ahead of me, I stopped in place and listened, somewhat startled. I did not hear anything going through the woods. My first thought was it was a hunter, then I thought it might be a weird person following me or something, so I started to get a little worried and thought of turning back toward my car. I tried to play back in my mind what I saw because it was somewhat of a blur when it happened. That's when I ruled out it was a person because it was all brown in color and had to be fur and not clothing. I knew it wasn't a deer because it was on two legs when it leaped across the trail. It was definitely a human shape though. After some thought I decided to proceed forward up the trail where I saw this thing cross. I had a 40 inch metal snake hook with me that I thought I could use if I needed to. When I got to the place I thought it crossed I looked through the thick trees to see if I could see anything but I did not. I resumed my snake hunting on the trail but I was looking over my shoulder the rest of the way. I returned back the trail a couple of hours later and did not see anything. I have to say it wasn't till I returned to my hotel room in Mt. Pleasant that I seriously thought what I saw might be something out of the ordinary.

October 20, 2004—I was traveling down Hwy 402 in Berkeley County going to load some steel at a steel plant. It was just before dark and I saw something ahead on all fours crossing the road. At first I thought it was a horse, then a bear. It did not have a natural gait and the body was too thin to be a horse and it was too tall to be a bear. As I closed up on it I saw that it had dark brown hair that was several inches long. The head was smaller than a horse or a bear. I believe it to be a Bigfoot on all fours. I had slowed down and stopped where I thought it had gone into the woods. It was very thick at this point. Standing, it would probably be 9 feet tall from my opinion.

January 2007—I deliver newspapers early in the morning. I was almost finished with the route and I made a left turn on to [edited] *and placed a paper in the tube. I proceeded to the next tube, and after placing the paper in it, my headlights caught something off to the far left. I observed a figure walking along the tree line along the edge of the cornfield away from my position. At first I thought it might be a man, but it was all black and it turned and I saw large red eyes staring back. I could not make out its face, and it continued to walk away. I turned my vehicle in past the paper tube to try and get a better look. It was at this point it stopped and looked at my direction again. From my estimation it looked to be at least 75 to 100 yards away, and about 6 or 7 feet tall. The creature then continued walking away, and feeling spooked I drove out of there fast. I proceeded to finish my paper route, trying to comprehend what I had just seen. It was just starting to become lighter out, it was about 6:45am, and it was still quite dark out. This area has a lot of farmland and wooded areas, and is very rural. The whole incident occurred in about 20 or 25 seconds. I felt as if I might have disturbed "it," for I felt an uneasy feeling when it looked my way. As this is the country, I see a lot of wildlife out at night when I deliver papers—deer, foxes, raccoons, possum, and even bobcat. I have hiked and spent lots of time in the Appalachians and I know what a bear looks like and have seen bear up close during hikes on the Appalachian Trail. I know there are some bear in South Carolina, but they mostly reside in the upper part of the state. What I saw definitely was not a bear.*

The colonists may have been able to drive the Cherokees from Berkeley County, but apparently there are some things that just won't leave the swamps. Perhaps Kecleh-Kudleh is one of them.

THE CHEROKEE LEGEND OF SPEAR FINGER

The Cherokees avoided the Little People and Kecleh-Kudleh, but sometimes other beings were malicious and had to be dealt with. Most southeastern tribes believed that each individual had a spirit and could become a ghost after death. Ghosts could make themselves visible to whomever they chose, but oftentimes they remained invisible. When a person died, the village shouted and made noise to drive the ghost away. If the ghost was allowed to stay, it would drain the energy from the living and cause illness or even death. Sometimes ghosts would get lonely and come back and visit relatives not realizing that they were bringing illness. They, too, had to be driven away.

Sometimes a murdered man whose death was not avenged would come back and haunt the eaves of his own house until his equal blood was shed by the murderer or his family. Ghosts were not tolerated well. Neither were witches. Conjuring and magic were generally accepted as everyday occurrences to the Cherokees. What they could not stand were those who abused it. They had a very low tolerance for witches.

One such person was known as Spear Finger. She was an old hag who lived off human livers. They became her sole source of nourishment. Spear Finger was also a shape-shifter and could take any form, although her favorite was that of a helpless and harmless old woman. Spear Finger also cast a spell on herself that made her skin as hard as rock. This made her invincible to spears and arrows. Even the sharpest knife could not cut the old witch.

Spear Finger had one identifying characteristic that she tried to keep concealed. That was a long forefinger. The finger was pure bone and resembled an awl or a spear. She used it to stab anyone she could get close enough to. Her favorite pastime was to walk along the trails where children picked blackberries. She would coax them in a sweet voice by saying, "Come grandchildren, come to granny and let her fix your hair." Inevitably, some young girl would come over and lay her head on the old woman's lap, and the old witch would play with her hair until the child fell asleep. She would then stab the sleeping child through the heart or the back of the neck with the long bony finger that she kept hidden under her robe. She would then cut out the dead child's liver and eat it.

After many children disappeared, a great council was called together to figure out what to do about Spear Finger. Soon they devised a plan to dig a large pit along the path and conceal the pit with underbrush. When the witch would step on the underbrush, she would fall into the pit and not be able to escape. The warriors would then attack her in unison.

Spear Finger did indeed fall into the trap. The hunters and warriors rushed to the pit and began trying to kill the witch. Well the arrows and spears had no effect on her stony skin and just bounced off. The warriors kept firing until they were almost exhausted. A little bird, a titmouse, was perched on a tree high above and watched what was taking place. The bird cried out "heart," and the warriors took its advice and began shooting at the witch's heart—still to no effect. In frustration, a warrior grabbed the titmouse and cut off its tongue.

Soon another bird, a chickadee, flew down from a tree and landed on the witch's right hand. The warriors took this as a sign that they should aim for the witch's hand. The witch had been motionless up until this moment, but now she began to jump about the pit and try and stab the warriors with her bony finger. The warriors continued firing at Spear Finger as she jumped about. Finally, one of the arrows struck her directly through the wrist of her right hand, the hand that held the deadly finger. The witch then fell over and bled to death from her wound. She had cast a spell of protection on her entire body except for the hand that held her spear-like finger. It was her only weakness, and a tiny little bird guided the warriors to it.

Spear Finger is a legend that has traveled with the Cherokees wherever they went. She was said to roam the mountains of Cherokee, North Carolina, while others claim she followed the Cherokees to Oklahoma. Others claimed to set the record straight: she was a vile evil being that gained her powers from demonic forces. She used those powers to appear when and where she wanted. She hid her hand and her secret weakness from all until the little chickadee figured it out. This is allegedly the origin of the phrase "a little birdie told me."

The Ghosts of Camp Low Country and Richmond Plantation

In the mid-1760s, Colonel John Harleston purchased Richmond Plantation. Legend has it that Colonel Harleston was almost unable to buy the property because he was thrown from his horse while crossing a bridge, and his money, which was bills of credit from the Province, was soaked in the river. He attempted to dry the money on the side of the road, but a gust of wind blew it back into the water. He jumped in to retrieve the bills and rode off to Richmond Plantation, arriving just before the purchase deadline.

Harleston soon added Villa Plantation, Bossis Plantation and Rice Hope Plantation, as well as land and another home on the Charleston peninsula, to his landholdings. Richmond Plantation, however, was his country seat. From there, he represented the parish of Saint John's Berkeley.

Long after Colonel Harleston's swim and purchase of the plantation, 153 acres of Richmond Plantation have belonged to the Girl Scouts of Eastern South Carolina. Since that purchase in 1963, the area has been known as Camp Low Country and has created many fond memories for many young ladies throughout the years. It also may have created a scare or two.

Many of the tales handed down through the ranks of Girl Scouts through the decades may have quite possibly been fabricated for the sheer fun of scaring one another—then again, maybe not.

One of the stories involves a young girl named Alice who had a beautiful white horse. The horse was a trained jumper and performed very well under the watchful eye of the young girl's father. The young girl enjoyed her time with the horse, yet the horse had a wild streak that only seemed to be kept in control by the stern commands of the young lady's father.

One day, Alice, against her father's directions, took the horse out on her own. The horse, realizing that the stern master was not around, displayed his wild streak to the fullest. After racing around frenetically and uncontrollably, he began to buck and rear. Poor Alice was sent flying through the air. The helpless girl struck a tree, and her neck was broken. She died instantly.

Many a Girl Scout has reported seeing Alice riding a white horse across the grounds of Richmond Plantation. They are often seen under the moonlit sky racing across the fields. Alice is also said to return and speak to the young Scouts, advising them of the importance of listening to their parents and telling them that she is an excellent example of what might happen to you if you choose not to listen.

Another young apparition is that of Jeannie, who haunts a little playhouse on the plantation. The house has been set up just as it used to be, but it has been sealed off from entry. Jeannie used to have wonderful imaginary tea parties there until one day, when she accidentally broke a piece of the china she was using and cut herself badly. Before she could even get out of the playhouse, she bled to death. They say that on moonlit nights you can look into the little playhouse and see the blood running down the walls.

Also on the plantation, there is said to be a large tiger-colored tabby cat with bright, gleaming eyes. He is said to disappear and reappear much like the Cheshire Cat in *Alice's Adventures in Wonderland.*

In addition to those is a gentleman who is the grandfather of a little boy who drowned in the duck pond there. He is said to have died from grief after the death of the child, and he can be seen walking the roads searching for the boy.

Just like the grounds of the property, the old house is said to have its fair share of ghostly activity, too. Lights turn themselves off and on, and rocking chairs rock and stop all by themselves.

LOCH DHU PLANTATION

The Kirks, a very prominent South Carolina family, settled Loch Dhu Plantation in St. John's Parish. The name is a Scottish-Gaelic term meaning "black lake," and the plantation was named for just such a pond located on the property.

During the Civil War, Dr. Philip Sidney Kirk served as a surgeon for the Confederate forces. Loch Dhu served as a makeshift hospital and was used to nurse injured Confederate soldiers back to health. When Union troops arrived in the South, they generally burned everything in their path. Loch Dhu was no exception to the orders, and when the Union troops arrived there, they intended to do the same—except the Kirk women refused to leave.

The Kirk women had become nurses to the injured Confederate soldiers and refused to leave. No amount of threats and coercion could dissuade them from their duties. In a rare change of heart, the Union troops decided not to forcibly remove the women and did not burn the plantation or any of its building. Loch Dhu was spared.

When the lands were flooded to create the lakes for the Santee Cooper Project, Loch Dhu survived. The house was on higher ground than its neighboring plantations. Much like the Wampee House survived Lake Moultrie, so did Loch Dhu survive Lake Marion. Also, just as Wampee House seems to be the focal point for the spirits disturbed by the creation of Lake Moultrie, Loch Dhu seems to be the gathering point for those disturbed by Lake Marion.

The Loch Dhu plantation house. *Courtesy of Library of Congress Archives.*

According to some folks, the doors of Loch Dhu often open and close on their own, and heavy boot steps can still be heard echoing up and down the stairs of the plantation house and throughout the upstairs hallways. The boot steps are believed to be those of the Union troops still trying to persuade the Kirk women to leave the home. The boot steps continue as they follow the women in and out of the rooms as they continue to care for the Confederate soldiers in a war that ended more than a century ago.

CONCLUSION

The ghost tales and folklore of Berkeley County are as diversified as the cultures that blended together to form the county. By no means is this a complete collection. There are about as many tales as there were plantations. Likewise, just as numerous plantations were lost with the creation of Lakes Marion and Moultrie with the Santee Cooper Project in the 1930s, so are the legends and lore being lost as well.

For example, Old Fannie at Middleburg Plantation and the Cordesville Conductor are two more examples of spook lights in the Berkeley County area. Old Fannie is said to be the spirit of one of the plantation's former slaves. She is said to dress in white, and every Friday night she wanders the long road to the plantation house in Huger, South Carolina, carrying a torch. The Cordesville Conductor is said to be the spirit of a man killed while working for the railroad in Cordesville, South Carolina. He is said to have fallen between two moving boxcars and decapitated. He takes his lantern and wanders the tracks nightly in search of the head that was never found. Both of these apparitions, much like the Summerville Light, are said to appear in the form of a glowing sphere of light. There is not a whole lot of information regarding the background of these apparitions, but it does show additional examples and the prevalence of the phenomena known as spook lights in the Berkeley County area.

Daniel Island supposedly had an apparition of a mounted British soldier riding through the island. I don't know where—when it was recorded in a two-sentence paragraph in a book decades ago, they failed to mention that part. That tale has forever faded into obscurity due to the fact that it was never properly written down and because the ones who told the tale have long passed on. This is why *Ghosts of Berkeley County, South Carolina* was created.

APPENDIX

A Word to Would-Be Ghost Hunters and Artifact Collectors

Once again, as I stated in the introduction, I offer these tales as entertainment, and I will take no stand on the existence, or nonexistence, of any of the paranormal denizens of Berkeley County (Summerville Light excluded). If one chooses to investigate these locations and chase a ghost, a Cymbee or Sasquatch, one chooses to do so on his or her own. Amateur ghost hunting seems thrilling, but there are numerous things to consider before undertaking such an endeavor. First and foremost is seeking permission to be on a particular site. Many areas, such as Strawberry Chapel, are posted with "no trespassing" signs and are under video surveillance due to the severe amount of vandalism the place has experienced throughout the years. If you trespass there, you will be prosecuted. I was fortunate enough to run into a groundskeeping crew the last time I was there, and I was allowed to look around. I am sure that other locations, such as the Nazareth Cemetery, do not want people running through the graveyards late at night, either.

Sheep Island Road is completely blocked off from travel and is also posted with "no trespassing" signs. It is an isolated and dangerous area regardless of the existence of ghosts. In May 2003, a Summerville police officer was shot in a confrontation with a suspect on Sheep Island Road. Fortunately, his body armor stopped the round, and he survived. The fact is that the area is secluded and dangerous, and trying to locate the ghosts of the dead may cause you to be turned into one by the living.

Vandalism to the graves at the historic Strawberry Chapel. *Courtesy of KOP Shots.*

The plantations that remain, regardless of being inhabited or not, are owned by someone somewhere. Being in a building without permission is burglary in this state.

That is just the legal side of amateur ghost hunting. Running around in a graveyard late at night is ill-advised. Brown recluse spiders leave nasty bites—been there and done that. Black widows can kill you. So can rattlesnakes and copperheads, which love hunting at night. Again, you may become a ghost searching for ghosts.

The State of South Carolina requires a person to obtain a license from the South Carolina Institute of Archaeology and Anthropology to collect artifacts or fossils while diving in the state. One must report their discoveries quarterly in order to maintain their license. This accompanied by the fact of obtaining scuba certification can get you started as a hobby collector, but

Above: The author exploring the old foundation of Wadboo Bridge. Water moccasins and alligators can create hazards for freshwater divers in South Carolina. *Courtesy of Swamp Fox Diving.*

Below: Rick Presnell of Swamp Fox Diving. A state license is required for the underwater collection of fossils and historic artifacts. *Courtesy of Swamp Fox Diving.*

diving obviously has its own dangers. If you choose to dive Lake Moultrie in search of the sunken plantations described in this book, here is a little information you may want to consider. Water moccasins are territorial and deadly but are nothing compared to alligators. On September 16, 2007, fifty-nine-year-old Bill Hedden was snorkeling in the lake when he was attacked by a twelve-foot, 600-pound alligator, which ripped off his left arm. Five nurses who were at a picnic nearby were able to stop the bleeding until paramedics arrived. The alligator was killed, and Hedden recovered, but doctors at the Medical University of South Carolina were not able to reattach it. Another fact for consideration is that in September 2010, Maryellen Mara-Christian from Fitchburg, Massachusetts, bagged a thirteen-and-a-half-foot, 1,025-pound alligator in Lake Moultrie during the state's hunting season. It took about two hours to secure the gator.

During mating season, a bull gator blows bubbles under the chin of his intended love interest. When you are scuba diving, as you exhale through your regulator, you blow bubbles that rise upward to the surface. That fourteen-foot bull gator lingering up there may mistake you for some other bull gator fooling around with his girlfriend and may just charge in fighting and ask questions later.

Amateur ghost hunting and artifact collecting may seem fun, but there are risks. Just because some yo-yo accidentally snaps a picture of his thumb over the lens of his camera and gets excited at the blurry orb he created does not make that orb a ghost. Orbs do not equal ghosts…sorry. Don't let some amateur group with a whole lot of pricey toys sucker you in and get you hurt, arrested or killed chasing lightning bugs in a graveyard. Likewise, don't let some artifact hunter with a scuba mask get you drowned. Check credentials and references.

BIBLIOGRAPHY

Adams, Natalie P. "The Cymbee Water Spirits of St. John's Berkeley." The African Diaspora Archaeology Network newsletter, June 2007.

American Wars 101. "The American Revolutionary War, the Skirmishes at Quenby Bridge and Shubrick's Plantation." http://www.americanwars101.com/battles/810717a.html.

Bass, Robert D. *Swamp Fox: The Life and Campaigns of General Francis Marion.* Orangeburg, SC: Sandlapper Publishing Company, 1974.

Baxley, Sandra. "Ghostly Summerville Light Still Makes Nightly Rounds." *(Charleston) News and Courier*, November 12, 1970.

Beach, Virginia Christian. *Medway.* Charleston, SC: Wyrick and Company, 1999.

Bigfoot Field Researchers Organization (BFRO). Geographic Database of Bigfoot/Sasquatch Sightings and Reports. http://www.bfro.net/GDB.

Bostick, Douglas W. *Sunken Plantations: The Santee Cooper Project.* Charleston, SC: The History Press, 2008.

Brown, Dan. "Wampee House: A Haunted Place." *Berkeley Independent*, October 27, 2008.

Buxton, Geordie. *Haunted Plantations: Ghosts of Slavery and Legends of the Cotton Kingdoms.* Charleston, SC: Arcadia Publishing, 2007.

Chapman, J. Milling. *Red Carolinians.* Columbia: University of South Carolina Press, 1969.

Corkran, David H. *The Carolina Indian Frontier.* Columbia: University of South Carolina Press, 1970.

Cross, J. Russell. *Historic Ramblin's Through Berkeley.* Columbia, SC: R.L. Bryan Company, 1985.

Dahlman, Michael K. *Daniel Island.* Charleston, SC: Arcadia Publishing, 2006.

Fennell, Edward. "Ghostly Tales Abound in Berkeley County: Former School Teacher Keeps Records of Hauntings." *(Charleston) Post and Courier*, October 29, 2001.

Heitzler, Michael J. *Historic Goose Creek, South Carolina, 1670–1980.* Easley: South Carolina Southern Historical Press, 1983.

Legendre, Gertrude Sanford. *The Time of My Life.* Charleston, SC: Wyrick and Company, 1987.

Manley, Roger. *Weird Carolinas.* New York: Sterling Publishing Company, 2007.

Martin, Margaret Rhett. *Charleston Ghosts.* Columbia: University of South Carolina Press, 1963.

Nichols, Mary. "Watch Out! Halloween Is Almost Here." *Berkeley Democrat*, October 29, 1986.

Pinckney, Roger. *Blue Roots: African-American Folk Magic of the Gullah People.* Orangeburg, SC: Sandlapper Publishing Company, 2003.

Rhyne, Nancy. *Slave Ghost Stories: Tales of Hags, Hants, Ghosts, and Diamondback Rattlers.* Orangeburg, SC: Sandlapper Publishing Company, 2002.

Rose, Mrs. Arthur Gordon. *Little Mistress Chicken: A Veritable Happening of Colonial Carolina.* N.p.: National Society of Colonial Dames in America reprinting, 1993.

Shuler, William. *The Ole Days in Berkeley County, South Carolina.* Bloomington, IN: 1st Books/Authorhouse, 2002.

———. *Short Stories About Life in Berkeley County, South Carolina.* Bloomington, IN: Authorhouse, 2007.

South Carolina's Information Highway (SCIWAY). http://www.sciway.net.

Staff of John F. Blair Publishing Company, eds. *Boogers and Boo-Daddies: The Best of Blair's Ghost Stories.* Winston-Salem, NC: self-published, 2004.

Turnage, Sheila. *Haunted Inns of the Southeast.* Winston-Salem, NC: John F. Blair, Publisher, 2002.

Walsh, Norman Sinkler. *Plantations, Pineland Villages, Pinopolis and Its People.* Virginia Beach, VA: Donning Company Publishers, 2006.

Wikipedia. "Berkeley County, South Carolina." http://en.wikipedia.org/w/index.php?title=Berkeley_County,_South_Carolina&oldid=425088703.

———. "Huguenot." http://en.wikipedia.org/w/index.php?title=Huguenot&oldid=435938276.

———. "Jack Sprat." http://en.wikipedia.org/w/index.php?title=Jack_Sprat&oldid=423393061.

———. "Philip Simmons." http://en.wikipedia.org/w/index.php?title=Philip_Simmons&oldid=425896930.

Wilkerson, Lynn. *Slow Travels—South Carolina.* N.p.: Caddo Publications, 2010.

Wilson, Robert. *Half Forgotten By-Ways of the Old South.* Columbia, SC: State Company, 1928.

About the Author and Photographer

Bruce Orr was raised in the Lowcountry of South Carolina and grew up hunting and fishing the plantations of Berkeley County with his father and brothers. It was during those times that he spent many evenings listening to the tales and legends surrounding this historic area. As a young boy, he had an insatiable appetite for the bizarre, unexplained and paranormal and was always searching for answers behind the events he heard at the hunt clubs and fish camps.

As he grew into an adult, this natural curiosity in seeking the facts brought him into law enforcement, where he eventually became a detective and a supervisor within his agency's Criminal Investigative Division. Now retired, he uses the skills he obtained in his career to research the legends and lore that he grew up with in order to record and preserve them for future generations.

Kayla Orr became interested in photography at a very young age. She studied photography throughout her high school curriculum and, at the age of sixteen, created KOP Shots, her own amateur photography company. Professionally, *Ghosts of Berkeley County, South Carolina* is the third book featuring her work, and she is currently working on an inspirational project that will combine her love of nature and photography.

Photo by Tiffany Baur.

Visit us at
www.historypress.net